Predatory Publishing

Predatory Publishing introduces and examines many forms of unethical and unprofessional publishing, whilst also analyzing its tactics and impact on scholarly communication.

Covering all aspects of predatory publishing, including topics such as predatory journals, hijacked publications, alternative metrics, and fraudulent conferences, the book considers the sociocultural, geopolitical, and technical impact of predatory behaviors. Demonstrating that predatory publishing has taken advantage of the open access movement, the author highlights the negative impact such publishing practices have had on science discovery and dissemination around the world. Efforts to counter unethical and destructive conduct, such as journal blacklists, peer-review sting operations, the implementation of the strict journal selection criteria by the Directory of Open Access Journals, and government regulations in some countries, are also fully described.

Predatory Publishing is a useful resource for every researcher, practitioner, and student in the global scholarly community. Individuals can expect to get a whole picture of the practice by reading this book, and decision-makers will find it informative to support their decisions. This book will be of interest to those studying and working in the fields of publishing, library and information science, communication science, economics, and higher education. People in other fields, particularly biomedical sciences, will also find it useful.

Jingfeng Xia is an independent researcher. He previously served as Dean of Library, Collections, and Online Education at East Stroudsburg University of Pennsylvania, and a tenured professor in the School of Informatics and Computing at Indiana University in Indianapolis. His research areas include open access publishing, institutional repositories, and Geographic Information Systems for libraries.

Predatory Publishing

Jingfeng Xia

LONDON AND NEW YORK

Cover: Getty Images

First published 2022
by Routledge
4 Park Square, Milton Park, Abingdon, Oxon OX14 4RN

and by Routledge
605 Third Avenue, New York, NY 10158

Routledge is an imprint of the Taylor & Francis Group, an informa business

© 2022 Jingfeng Xia

The right of Jingfeng Xia to be identified as author of this work has been asserted in accordance with sections 77 and 78 of the Copyright, Designs and Patents Act 1988.

All rights reserved. No part of this book may be reprinted or reproduced or utilised in any form or by any electronic, mechanical, or other means, now known or hereafter invented, including photocopying and recording, or in any information storage or retrieval system, without permission in writing from the publishers.

Trademark notice: Product or corporate names may be trademarks or registered trademarks, and are used only for identification and explanation without intent to infringe.

British Library Cataloguing-in-Publication Data
A catalogue record for this book is available from the British Library

Library of Congress Cataloging-in-Publication Data
A catalog record for this book has been requested

ISBN: 978-0-367-46532-2 (hbk)
ISBN: 978-1-032-22454-1 (pbk)
ISBN: 978-1-003-02933-5 (ebk)

DOI: 10.4324/9781003029335

Typeset in Times New Roman
by Apex CoVantage, LLC

Contents

	List of figures	vi
	List of tables	vii
	Acknowledgement	viii
1	Introduction	1
2	Background	5
3	Journals	12
4	Publishers	39
5	Stakeholders	59
6	Hijacked publishing	75
7	Conferences	91
8	Metrics and indexes	105
9	Conclusion	113
	Appendix A Slightly modified Beall's third version of criteria for predatory behaviors	116
	Appendix B Cabells's criteria for predatory practices, version 1.1	118
	References	123
	Index	142

Figures

3.1 Screenshot of a conversation between a commenter and Jeffrey Beall   15
3.2 Increase of journals in DOAJ by year   21
3.3 Top ten languages used by DOAJ journals   22
3.4 Top ten countries where DOAJ journals are published   22
3.5 Journal overlaps between selected blacklists and whitelists   27
4.1 Increase of predatory publishers over time   40
4.2 Screenshot of announcement for adding new publishers to the blacklist   40
4.3 Screenshot of Beall's instructions for appeals   41
6.1 Website of the legitimate journal *Sylwan* (A) and its hijacked English version (B)   85
6.2 The journal *Afinidad* and its information, available on SCImago   86
7.1 Logo of Think.Check.Attend   103

Tables

3.1	Number of standalone journals by year	14
3.2	Numbers of journals on Cabells's blacklist by year	18
3.3	Journal ranks in JQL	25
3.4	A selected list of crowd-sourced services	26
3.5	Size of journals and their total number of articles in 2015	30
3.6	Numbers and percentages of predatory journals and articles by segment in 2015	30
3.7	APC rates in US dollars	31
3.8	Common prefixes of predatory journal titles	34
3.9	Numbers of journals disappeared by year	35
4.1	Top ten countries with predatory publications in 2015	44
4.2	Numbers of special issues by selected MDPI journals as of early 2021	49
4.3	The face value of the APC rates by OMICS's journals in US dollars	51
5.1	Top ten countries with predatory authors	61
5.2	Top five countries of predatory authors in economics	62
5.3	Country proportions of editors serving journals by the Science Publishing Group	69
6.1	Examples from a hijacked journal list	79
6.2	Features to identify hijacked journals	87
7.1	List of indicators of predatory conferences	93
8.1	Examples of artificial metrics	108
8.2	Examples of alternative indexes	110

Acknowledgement

This is a long-delayed project due to personal reasons. The delay, however, gave me time to read much more literature on the subject that only became available recently. I felt lucky to find interesting studies that would not yet have been published if this book were completed on time, but also realized that I would become overwhelmed by the huge number of new publications if I kept waiting for more discoveries.

I would like to thank Heidi Lowther of Routledge and her team for their patience and useful instructions. I also want to thank the four reviewers who have provided constructive suggestions for improving the book. However, I am solely responsible for any mistakes, errors, and opinions in the manuscript. My son, David, helped polish the final draft, and my wife encouraged me to move forward with the project. Their assistance is appreciated. In writing the book, I discussed my progress with many people, such as Van Reidhead and Trib Puri, both of whom are professors at East Stroudsburg University. I thank them for their support.

I am grateful to *Knowledge E* and Cabells for granting me permissions to use their materials. Both Emily Choynowski and Simon Linacre extended their help so I could include the Think.Check.Attend logo and Cabells's criteria of predatory practices in the book. I also want to thank Jeffrey Beall, who gave me permission to use his 2015 criteria for determining predatory practices in the appendix with slight reformatting. I appreciate their kindness.

1 Introduction

This book seeks to illustrate the dynamics of predatory publishing and serve as a reference point to help readers become familiar with primary predatory practices. Predatory publishing is an exploitative business model in the scholarly publishing market that is devised solely for financial gain (Beall, 2013). It sets article processing charges (APCs) for authors, provides no or only peripheral peer reviews for submissions, and ignores editorial services for publications (Anderson, 2019). To maximize profit, predatory publishers often adopt deceptive tactics to entice submissions and compel payments. The definition of predatory publishing, devised by a group of researchers, publishers, policymakers, funders, and librarians from ten countries, is:

> [publications] that prioritize self-interest at the expense of scholarship and are characterized by false or misleading information, deviation from best editorial and publication practices, a lack of transparency, and/or the use of aggressive and indiscriminate solicitation practices.
> (Grudniewicz *et al.*, 2019)

Aside from this concise definition, detailed criteria to identify predatory publishing have been developed and frequently adjusted by scholars or organizations to capture diverse and constantly changing practices (Strinzel *et al.*, 2019). The first comprehensive criteria were assembled by Jeffrey Beall in 2012, that include 48 signs of predatory practices which were amended in 2015 to increase to 54 signs, falling in four categories: editors and staff, integrity, business management, and other (Beall, 2012, 2015). Similar criteria have been made by others, e.g., Cobey *et al.* (2018), Cukier *et al.* (2020), and Eriksson and Helgesson (2017). All criteria aim to assess journals and publishers by measuring every aspect of their function, from the evaluation of their publication quality to the observation of their abnormal operations, but differ in individual measures (e.g., Olivarez *et al.*, 2018).

DOI: 10.4324/9781003029335-1

2   *Introduction*

Predatory publishing has become an epidemic practice over the past two decades. The earliest evidence was noted in the late 2000s, when publishers started sending spam emails to individual researchers to solicit submissions and invite them to serve as editors or on editorial boards (Beall, 2009; Eysenbach, 2008; Poynder, 2008). These publications were found to lack transparency, be exploitative, and not check content for quality and legitimacy (Beall, 2013). Beall applied his criteria to identify a list of possible predatory publishers, and published the list on his website scholarlyoa.org in the early 2010s. He subsequently added a list of standalone journals and some other lists. These lists immediately became popular as the go-to tools to help authors avoid predatory outlets, though controversy surrounding the accuracy of inclusions remained (Kendall, 2021; Teixeira da Silva, 2017).

Since then, predatory publishing has grown exponentially. Beall listed 18 predatory publishers in 2010, while the number climbed to 1,163 in early 2017, when he shut down his website. A study by Björk *et al.* (2020) found more than 10,000 predatory journals in 2018, which is a stark contrast to the fewer than 100 journals in the earliest journal blacklist (Beall, 2013). Similarly, the total number of articles in predatory journals increased from 53,000 in 2010 to an estimated 420,000 in 2014 (Shen & Björk, 2015). These volumes indicate the involvement of hundreds of thousands of scholars across the world in predatory publishing.

Predatory publishing is a heterogenous mixture of businesses, which is not only reflected in varied practices in editorial and publishing services, but also in multiple forms of publishing outcomes. Its most popular form is dishonourable scholarly journals by predatory publishers, but it also includes predatory conferences, hijacked journals, and artificial metrics and alternative indexes. Authors who get involved in predatory publishing include scholars who fall prey to spam invitations and those who are knowing participants for personal reasons (Perlin *et al.*, 2018).

The literature of predatory publishing has been distributed across all scientific disciplines, particularly in health science (Mertkan *et al.*, 2021). Studies are mostly discipline-specific and can hardly paint a big picture of the practice. Insofar as we can tell, there is no single manuscript which synthesizes the scattered studies and observations on the business, but researchers do need a comprehensive guide that is international in scope to assist those from both developing and developed countries who have been victimized by, or have intentionally participated in, predatory publishing. Hopefully, this book will also help the general public understand the complexity of academic misconduct, since the results of low-quality and fraudulent scientific studies can negatively impact practice, perceptions, and decision-making.

Introduction 3

The harm of predatory practices to scholarship is tangible. Publishing in predatory outlets is a waste of effort, time, and money, since it will not add any scientific merits to the authors, as indicated by the negligible citation counts (Björk *et al.*, 2020; Moher *et al.*, 2017). At the same time, it can damage the reputation of individuals, institutions, and funding agencies. The best way to fight predatory publishing is to promote awareness among people – including those in the Global South, where access to scholarly information is not always available and those in the North, where pressure to publish has been enormous – by providing a single point of introduction that brings all the many issues together. This is what the book hopes to achieve.

About this book

This book introduces the primary forms of predatory publishing, focusing on both the tactics and the results. It views predatory publishing as a scholarly ecosystem of the open access (OA) movement, reviews it on a global scale, and pinpoints its negative impact on science discovery and dissemination. Efforts to fight unprofessional and destructive conducts are described, and suggestions for avoiding predatory publishing are provided.

After this introductory chapter and the next chapter examining possible causes behind predatory publishing, Chapter 3 focuses on the key characteristics of predatory journals, including an introduction of the history and conditions of journal blacklists and whitelists and a summary of the studies on predatory journals. This chapter strives to describe the impact of scientific misconduct on scholarly communication, and attempts to provide tips as to what can be done to minimize involvement in predatory publishing.

Chapter 4 discusses predatory publishers that have been exposed for delivering false information to attract business. An analysis of the changes of blacklisted publishers is made to illustrate the development of predatory behaviors. Legal cases against and by predatory publishers are highlighted to delineate challenges in the fight against dishonorable and fraudulent practices.

The next chapter reviews the authorship of predatory publications: who has collaborated with predatory journals? Are they willing participants or innocent victims? It examines author profiles for their geographic distributions, academic ranking, publication history, and citation count. This chapter also explores the editorship of predatory journals to find how the journals adopt unethical techniques to trick scholars or steal personal identities, and how some scholars collude with publishers to build their credentials. Other roles in predatory publishing, namely those who help review submissions and those who read and cite articles in predatory journals, are all discussed.

In Chapter 6, hijacked publishing is introduced as an emerging type of cybercrime that impersonates legitimate academic journals by abusing or copying legitimate journal names and using logos from genuine publications to gain credibility. The hijacked websites and their attempts to intercept money from authors are highlighted. Some typical cases and detection strategies are described here.

Chapter 7 introduces various aspects of predatory conferences, which are the primary form of revenue for many predatory publishers. Predatory conferences are particularly common in health sciences, e.g., pharmaceutical sciences, and thus may potentially create negative impacts on the medical field. Both research results and media reports are synthesized to help readers understand the threat of pseudoscience and nonsense to scientific exploration as well as to our everyday lives.

The last chapter discusses predatory services that provide artificial impact factor values to questionable OA journals. The artificial metrics are compared to the standard metrics that have been recognized by the scholarly community. A list of artificial metrics as well as journal indexes is analyzed against well-recognized ones, revealing unethical conduct that takes advantage of open access to make profit for predatory services.

Predatory publishing is a very diverse practice that touches almost every facet of scholarly communication. Studies of, and opinions on, the practice are enormous, in various formats, and cover multiple academic fields. The complexity makes it difficult for the author to cover everything about the practice in one book. Nor does he intend to itemize all discoveries and opinions of each publication about the subject. It is inevitable that he has brought his personal views into the descriptions.

There has been debate over the term "predatory," which is considered unable to reflect the diverse practices of the field (e.g., Anderson, 2015). In many publications, predatory praxis is called "publishing crime," while actions to catch predation are labelled "academic witch-hunts" (Molchanova et al., 2017; Umlauf & Mochizuki, 2018). In other cases, the term is urged to be retired and be replaced with "write-only," "deceptive," "bad faith," "trash," and the like. This book, however, keeps the existing vocabulary because "predatory publishing" has been an extensively accepted label to define the practice.

2 Background

Predatory publishing does not come out of nowhere. Its arrival and bloom in popularity are the result of a combination of changes in scholarly pursuits, technological innovations, cultural norms, economic growth, and geopolitical shifts. Its commercial success and academic damage need to be explored in a historical context. A thorough examination of the interrelationship between predatory publishing and related influential factors is beyond both the scope of this book and the capability of the author. This book presents the most relevant topics pertinent to the creation and growth of predatory publishing, and offers only a concise introduction.

2.1 The provenance of predatory publishing

The model of pay-to-publish by authors is considered one of the root causes of predatory publishing (Berger, 2017). It is a business model that can be traced back two centuries, known as vanity publishing or self-publishing (Laquintano, 2013). In the beginning, publishers relied on author subsidies to support poets, artists, and other first-time authors who did not have the necessary reputations, and to support manuscripts that possessed scientific or literary values but could not yield a return on the investment (Putnam, 1897). Up to the twentieth century, vanity publishing slowly developed into a lucrative and robust business and started amassing a reputation for deception (Dyrud, 2014; Sullivan, 1958).

With vanity publishing, authors pay to publish their work either in money or in publication rights. A vanity press usually publishes any book received without providing peer review or editorial services. Such books can be non-academic, such as recipes or photo albums, as well as scholarly in nature, e.g., theses and dissertations by junior academicians (Stromberg, 2014). These books can be made available through self-publishing outlets; and authors are often asked to buy a substantial number of copies of their book to help vanity presses increase revenue and aid authors themselves in promoting their work.

People connect vanity publishing to predatory publishing because of their similarities in many areas of practice (Brown, 2015; Krawczyk & Kulczyki, 2021). However, there are several differences between the two. First, vanity presses do not claim to offer peer review, while predatory publishers do, although it is almost always a false avowal. Second, publications by the former are typically in a book format, although multimedia products have also been made recently, while the latter are mostly scholarly journals. Third, the content of vanity publications is not freely accessible on the web, though online marketing has become the norm, while predatory publications are all open access (OA). The strongest evidence to show that vanity publishing may not be a direct influence on predatory publishing is their chronological gap. Although vanity publishing predates online publishing, predatory publishing did not emerge immediately after OA journals started in the early 1990s, and only started to flourish in the early 2000s. Looking into developments in this period will help discover the real cause of predatory publishing.

It is the funding model of some OA journals developed in the early 2000s, i.e., the article processing charge (APC) model, that was introduced by several renowned OA publishers such as BioMed Central and the Public Library of Science (PLOS) to defray the cost of maintaining free access to scientific publications (Kutz, 2002; Quint, 2002). APCs are designed to be paid by individual authors, their institutions, or their research funders. Over the years, many government agencies and institutions have developed policies to support OA publishing by implementing policies to help pay for APCs. For example, a group of UK research funding organizations, with the support of the European Commission and the European Research Council, launched a Plan S initiative to make full and immediate open access of research publications a reality (coalition-s.org). This development reflects the continuous growth of OA and the acceptance of the APCs practice by the market.

OA is a revolutionized model of scholarship dissemination that seeks to make research outputs available to readers at no cost, in contrast to the traditional model that asks readers to access scholarly information by paying for a subscription (Suber, 2015). While there are many variations of OA publishing, the gold OA is the most relevant one, which provides free access to all of a publisher's articles via its platform (Björk *et al.*, 2010). Many gold OA journals charge APCs to authors. Open access started around the early 1990s, when the "serials crisis" intensified. "Serials crisis" describes the situation facing libraries and scholars where the increasing cost of journal subscriptions had dramatically outpaced the meager increases, if not decreases, of library budgets (Branin & Case, 1998). At the same time, researchers were also frustrated by the traditional model of scholarly communication

Background 7

that typically took years for research outcomes to be reviewed and published. A reform in journal publishing was in demand.

The rise and popularity of the internet made the reform possible. New forms of academic publishing were soon replacing print-based journal publishing, allowing innovative models to flourish in the market (Laakso et al., 2011; SQW, 2004). OA journals were created accordingly. In the beginning, OA journals were financially supported by research institutions, government grants, or by individuals volunteering contributions. They were completely free to readers as well as authors. The subsidized gold OA, however, was soon proven to be unsustainable when grant money ran out or when the operational agency could no longer afford its ongoing cost. Consequently, an author-pays funding system emerged to uphold the business (Houghton, 2010).

In a short span of time, APC-based publishing has become a popular operation. As of 2010, it was discovered that over 26% of OA journals in the Directory of Open Access Journals (DOAJ) set an APC requirement (Solomon & Björk, 2012). As of Spring 2021, DOAJ contained over 16,000 titles, of which 28% were APC-funded. DOAJ is referred to as the whitelist that provides access to self-registered, high-quality, and peer-reviewed OA journals, which consist of only a small portion of all OA journals in practice.

The fiscal success of the APC model has introduced fresh business opportunities to the publishing market. Unlike traditional publishing, which entails costs in such areas as editing, manufacturing, marketing, overhead, and distribution, OA publishing relies on ubiquitous internet and web technologies to be much more affordable (Xia, 2019). APC earnings have generated ample revenue, so academic publishing is no longer the exclusive business of major commercial publishers or public organizations. As a result, the market in the late 2000s and onward witnessed a rapid growth of new publishers and publications that adopted the APC operations (Budzinski et al., 2020).

Unlike reputable APC-based journals, many new journals and publishers have set profit as their sole goal. They attempt to maximize net profit by reducing every possible cost (Armstrong, 2014). For example, charges on editing services have been cut off; operations have been minimized into a one-person task; and marketing has only consisted of email spamming. Most importantly, peer review has given way to the acceptance of all submissions. Such publishing is also characterized by the existence of different types of fraudulent information, all aimed at attracting submissions. Compared to reputable OA journals that take APCs but offer rigorous scholarly safeguarding, the latter operations have gone too far across ethical and academic boundaries and become a critical threat to scientific pursuits and scholarly communication. More than 90% of the OA journals listed on Jeffrey Beall's list of predatory journals have set APCs (Crawford, 2017).

2.2 Pressure on scholarly publishing

If the author-pays model motivated exploitative behaviors in scholarly publishing, the stress of publishing for academics has helped fertilize the business of predatory publishing. The publish-or-perish mantra has long been a major stressor, under which scholars feel pressured to publish their research in order to stay relevant and be successful within the academic community (de Rond & Miller, 2005). The publish-or-perish practice is so widespread and powerful that it has become the standard way of life for academics. Universities and research institutions use quantity of publications as a criterion during recruitments, evaluations of tenure and promotion, and decisions on awards and funding. On the bright side, it pushes scholars to focus on research advancement and filter out those who are not suitable for an academic career. On the other hand, the culture has created a quantity-quality imbalance, because the pressure may drive researchers into publishing more work, but with low scientific value, or even fabricated and fake publications (Miller *et al.*, 2010).

The publish-or-perish culture, with both its advantages and drawbacks, was brought and transplanted into the academic soil of developing countries by the modern globalization movement. Started in the late 1980s, a new wave of economic globalization has made the world a small village (Hirst *et al.*, 2009; Tomlinson, 1999). Where the cross-border trading and industrial activities have facilitated the interdependence of world economies, an information globalization, including technologies, and a cultural globalization, including publishing, followed. It was no coincidence that the late 1980s and early 1990s was exactly the time when the internet started serving scholarly publishing, and open access initiatives set precedents for competing with the traditional publishing enterprise.

When the publish-or-perish system was introduced to developing countries, it became immediately popular due to a variety of conditions (Qiu, 2010; van Dalen & Henkens, 2012). There are economic reasons, e.g., lack of infrastructure in some countries, and sociocultural causes, e.g., local culture with a higher level of tolerance of lower academic rigor in some areas than others. Also, centralized control may make a society more likely to create and enforce strong policies over the entire country through its institutional influences; hence, a geopolitical agenda may have played a key role in the local development of this pressure-based structure.

Several countries have been repeatedly found to be the hardest hit areas with respect to their numbers of predatory activities. India has the most predatory journals, publishers, and conferences, probably exceeding the total of all other countries (Garanayak & Ramaiah, 2019). Top performers also include Pakistan, Iran, etc. When the numbers of predatory authors and articles are taken into consideration, India, China, Indonesia, Nigeria, Malaysia, Turkey, South Africa, and Kazakhstan stand out (e.g., Nwagwu, 2016; Wallace & Perri, 2018; Xia *et al.*, 2015). Not coincidentally, these are exactly the countries where the publish-or-perish mentality has been most prevalent.

It becomes clear that stringent policies have helped nurture the publish-or-perish culture and intensified researchers' anxiety about publishing more articles. Most countries producing a large number of predatory authors have implemented harsh publishing policies, at both the government and institutional levels, that penalize those who have not been able to keep pace with publishing and incentivize those whose articles appear in academic journals. Because of the efforts of these countries in globalization, their policies are set in favor of international journals that are published in the English language, preferably indexed by the Web of Science (WoS). Unfortunately, many of these countries do not use English as their official language, and thus their researchers have difficulties writing publishable articles. Many of their researchers may not have a solid training in scientific investigation either.

- In Indonesia, many universities require their faculty to publish at least 10% of their publications in English. However, only less than 5% of Indonesians, and the academics, can write English proficiently (Kozok, 2017).
- In China, institutions pay scientists who publish in top international journals. The cash rewards can range from $30 USD to $165,000 USD for a paper published in a WoS indexed journal (Abritis & McCook, 2017; Quan *et al.*, 2017). People without international publications may face layoffs at some institutions.
- The South African government initiated a subsidy plan in 2005 to award around $7,000 USD for authors who publish in recognized journals, but the criteria to evaluate recognized publications are questionable (Hedding, 2019).
- In Nigeria, universities set requirements for their faculty to be promoted to senior levels only if they have published a certain proportion of articles in foreign journals (Adomi & Mordi, 2003; Omobowale *et al.*, 2014).
- The Kazakhstan government set a policy in the early 2010s to require all PhD students to publish in journals that are indexed by Scopus (Denisova-Schmidt, 2020, p. 53).

When academic publishing is strongly tied to performance assessments while regular scholars are short of training in language and scientific competencies, individuals have no choice but are impelled to take alternative paths. Predatory publications arose at the right time. Many Indian publishers, due to their language advantages over many other countries, a lax control over the publishing business by their government, and their own pressure to publish, took advantage of the internet, the APC model, and researchers' desire to publish in English language journals. Their deceitful and exploitive business caters to those from developing as well as developed countries for the chances to publish in foreign outlets.

2.3 Gatekeeping the quality of predatory publishing

Lack of peer review is referred to as one of the major characteristics of predatory publishing. Since the birth of the printing press, peer review has been an integral part of quality control (Biagioli, 2002; Spier, 2002). It was originally designed to filter out unqualified and dishonest submissions and help improve the content of manuscripts. In its simplest form, a peer review process starts from a research article being submitted to a scholarly journal, to the article being sent to experts in the field for evaluation. Upon reviews by the experts, the editor will decide whether to accept, reject, or return the submission to the author for revisions. The peer review tradition has been widely criticized for its defects, such as its slowness and possible bias (Kelly et al., 2014). Yet, before a better system is developed, peer review will still serve as the foundation of the publishing process for ensuring the credibility and quality of scholarly publications. It is still the standard practice of most valid scientific journals in the world.

It is always subjective to judge the quality of publications, and therefore difficult to attest to a lack of peer review in predatory publishing. All predatory journals claim to have conducted rigorous peer review. Over the years, researchers have developed alternate methods to test the nonexistence of peer review in predatory journals without directly evaluating the published articles.

Inspired by the renowned Sokal Affair, a hoax published in the journal *Social Text* in 1996, two authors in *Scholarly Kitchen*, a blog of the Society for Scholarly Publishing, utilized a computer program (SCIgen) to generate a nonsense paper and submitted it to a suspicious publisher in 2009 (Davis, 2009). Although this paper can easily be identified as a hoax by anyone even without the subject knowledge, it was still accepted for publishing. Upon acceptance, the authors retracted their submission and did not pay the requested APC of $800 USD. They cautiously point to the possible lack of peer review by this journal.

A large-scale sting operation exposed a widespread absence of gatekeeping by predatory journals (Bohannon, 2013). In this experiment, a research-like paper was crafted that did not have major problems in format and language, but had obviously flawed methodology and a meaningless conclusion that anyone with a high-school knowledge of the subject could detect. The author submitted this paper between January and August of 2013 to a group of 304 OA journals that asked for APCs. Of these journals, 167 journals were from DOAJ's whitelist, 121 appeared in Beall's blacklist, and 16 were listed by both.

By October 2013, 255 journals responded with a decision, of which 62% accepted the paper and 38% rejected it. Journals accepting it were mostly based in developing countries, mainly in India. A high 82% of journals from Beall's blacklist accepted the paper, as well as 45% of journals from the whitelist, revealing the appropriate selection of predatory titles by Beall and the questionable criteria of journal inclusions by DOAJ. In response to the findings, DOAJ adjusted its inclusion criteria (Olijhoek *et al.*, 2015). This sting operation revealed that the majority of tested journals did not show any sign of peer review, regardless of their claims.

Similar investigations have been conducted by others, not only for papers to OA journals, but also for submissions to scholarly conferences (e.g., Sample, 2014). Together, these stings are extensive enough to display the widespread presence of an easy acceptance by predatory publications. It is worth noting that exploitive behaviors and the ignorance of peer review are observed only on a subset of OA journals, and one should be careful about drawing a simple correlation between OA publishing and predatory practices. With the escalation of predatory publishing over the past decades, numerous online discussions and plentiful studies have been published to examine its various aspects of operations. The wide exposure has contributed to our understanding of predatory publishing.

3 Journals

This chapter covers the origins and primary characteristics of scholarly publications that are deemed predatory. It describes major journal blacklists and whitelists and their role in predatory publishing. It also provides tips for authors to avoid predatory publications, not only for naïve authors and readers, but also for anyone who wants to learn about the overall practice of predatory journals.

3.1 The beginning

Starting in the late 2000s, academicians frequently received unsolicited emails that invited them to serve as an editor or on the editorial boards or submit articles to the inviting journals (Beall, 2012). The spam emails praise the recipients and mention their previous publication(s), making them feel like they are specially treated, even though the rest of the email is just a template. The invitations appear more attractive to those who have the appetite for immediate academic visibility, such as junior scholars and those in developing countries, and so tend to welcome any opportunities that may sound promising. Many inviting journals have a title almost identical to that of established journals, which can easily trick people into believing that they are reading invitations from legitimate publications. The journals promise to turn submissions into formal publications within weeks, which is another compelling selling point.

Many people fall prey to the spam invitations and decide to cooperate with the journals, but it will take no time for them to regret their decisions. Once they agree to serve on editorship, they will be taken hostage and not be allowed to withdraw. When submissions are made and accepted, the authors will be immediately asked to pay an article processing charge (APC) that may not have been mentioned anywhere on the website or in communication with the editors. Other email recipients also grow suspicious due to the high frequency of invitations, their grammatical errors or obvious

DOI: 10.4324/9781003029335-3

typos, and subject coverage that are different from the recipients' area(s) of research, work, and knowledge (Moher & Srivastava, 2015).

The frequency of such invitations has remained relatively constant since its peak in 2008 (Beall, 2013). To evaluate the magnitude and nature of spam emails, one study decided to save all solicitations over a three-month period, and collected a total of 191 such emails from open access (OA) journals (Clemons *et al.*, 2017). At the same time, another study received 502 spam emails over a one-year window (Mercier *et al.*, 2017). Both are in the field of health sciences.

Many scholars have been overwhelmed by the amount of spam invitations and treat them as undesirable or unwanted emails. They choose to delete them and block the senders. One person did the opposite, however. Instead of simply deleting such emails, he decided to collect and analyze them. He went to the inviting journals' websites to examine their policies and ended up finding patterns of non-transparent practices that provide misleading information in order to draw submissions and charge APCs. By compiling a list of such publishers in 2010, he coined the term "predatory publisher." He then moved the list to his website scholarlyoa.org (now defunct), known as *Scholarly Open Access*, and expanded it two years later into two lists, one of publishers and the other of standalone journals. His name is Jeffrey Beall, a then-librarian at the University of Colorado in Denver, and his lists are widely referred to as Beall's lists or OA blacklists.

3.2 Blacklists of predatory journals

3.2.1 *Beall's blacklist of standalone predatory journals*

Several lists were maintained on scholarlyoa.org, among which the most popular ones were the blacklist for standalone journals and the blacklist containing the names of publishers, both of which were labelled as "potential, possible and probable" because of the pressure from critics who blamed Beall for jeopardizing the chance of start-up publishers to improve and grow. Titles on the first list were primarily journals operated independently by single-journal publishers, while publishers on the second list produce two or more journals. Because Beall never disclosed the titles of non-standalone journals, what is commonly referred to as the OA journal blacklist is the list of standalone journals.

With the creation of the journal blacklist, Beall posted on the same website his criteria for determining predatory practices. The early version of the criteria was distributed in August 2012; it was subsequently revised in December 2012, and then again in January 2015. The first version contained 48 criteria, while more items were added to the 2015 version, which is the

Table 3.1 Number of standalone journals by year

Year	# Journals
2013	126
2014	303
2015	507
2016	882
2017	1,294

Source: scholarlyoa.org

last version published (Appendix A). With the criteria, Beall identified a group of independent journals in early 2012, and the number kept growing each year. Table 3.1 copies statistics from his website. If all journals by the publishers on another list are counted and included, the total number of predatory journals was 11,873 as of 2014 (Shen & Björk, 2015).

The journal blacklist drew immediate attention. People around the world made their opinions available through media and publications to express their concerns about predatory practices, and also shared their discovery of dubious journals. Online and print discussions have been carried out by individuals, publishers, libraries, and institutions, in the form of commentaries, viewpoints, letters, editorials, and empirical studies. Such popularity has been helpful for educating academics, as well as the general public, about the facts and opinions of unprofessional and unethical publishing and behaviors. Beall's website was the center of discussion where readers left comments and provided information about specific suspicious titles, contributing to Beall's journal list. Figure 3.1 is a screenshot of a brief conversation between Beall and a commenter that helped add a predatory journal.

Some developed their own criteria. For example, Eriksson and Helgesson (2017) compiled a list of 25 signs of predatory journals. At the same time, Cobey *et al.* (2018) used a collection of 344 publications published between 2012 and 2018 on predatory journal identification to extract 109 unique characteristics of predatory publishing. They consolidated fragmented definitions and developed a consensus framework of what constitutes a predatory journal.

There is no major difference between Beall's criteria and others developed later, although they may contain slightly different measures or take distinct expressions and classifications. For example, what Beall categorized under the section of "business management" for hiding information about APCs is organized into the theme of "article processing charges" by Cobey *et al*. Eriksson and Helgesson added some new items, such as their measurement of a journal by seeing if it is unfamiliar to a

mi says:
November 7, 2016 at 7:28 PM

Academic Research Publishing Group is going start a new publication company : Noble Academic Publisher. Please click on that link : http://napublisher.org/?ic=fee&id=8. Company using the same name for payment.

Reply

> **Jeffrey Beall says:**
> November 8, 2016 at 12:16 PM
>
> Thanks. This publisher is now included on my list.
>
> Reply

Figure 3.1 Screenshot of a conversation between a commenter and Jeffrey Beall

reader and to the reader's colleagues. Nonetheless, the following three core characteristics have been agreed upon by the majority of, if not all, researchers:

1 Cheating behaviors that provide false and misleading information about business operations, such as editors and editorial teams, business location, etc., and about journals, such as their ranking, indexation, etc.
2 Ignoring, or providing fake to lax peer review, that results in low-quality or even fraudulent publications.
3 Asking an APC from authors.

Some measures in these criteria are hard to implement or prone to criticism. Regarding implementation, Eriksson and Helgesson (2017) admit that a journal may not necessarily be predatory if it meets only one of their criteria, "but the more points on the list that apply to the journal at hand, the more skeptical you should be" (p. 165). This makes identification of predatory journals arbitrary: how many points are considered adequate? Some measures do not appear solid; for example, Beall's assessment on the gender balance of editorial boards is not convincing.

Beall's efforts and products have drawn criticism, primarily of his criteria and his operations, as well as his personal stance on OA (e.g., Berger & Cirasella, 2015; Crawford, 2014; Teixeira da Silva, 2017; Teixeira da Silva & Al-Khatib, 2017). Harassments and legal threats by those publishers and journals whose names are included in the OA blacklists have been frequently made to Beall and his institution (Beall, 2017). Under massive pressure, Beall removed all the content from his website permanently in January 2017.

However, Beall's list of predatory journals has not completely gone away. The Internet Archive (archive.org) has preserved most updates of the list throughout history, thereby providing a great resource for anyone who is interested in its development. The last version of the blacklist is cloned by a PhD researcher at a European university on a new site, called beallslist.net. Also, this researcher continues to update the list using input from readers with over 1,500 entries in early 2021 which represents several hundreds more records. A similar job is done by a group of anonymous scholars and information professionals who rebuilt Beall's lists on predatoryjournals.com. This site allows everyone to make contributions, edits, and suggestions through a web format. As of early 2021, the site had a total of 1,317 titles.

The cloned blacklists inherit Beall's criteria and journal entries. Their creators make it clear that they do not have the necessary time and energy to focus on continuous updates. To avoid any possible harassment and threats, they have decided to remain anonymous. As a result, people do not see much accountability in the work when nobody takes responsibility for it, and so, feel difficult to rely on the updates. To some extent, Beall's list has become a time capsule. Another blacklist that carries on Beall's effort but makes commendable revisions to Beall's criteria is Cabells's blacklist, also known as the Journal Blacklist. Its name was recently changed to Predatory Reports.

3.2.2 Cabells's blacklist of predatory journals

The sudden unavailability of Beall's journal blacklist caught many academics off guard because they had increasingly counted on it as the *de facto* standard to identify faulty publications, thus creating a vacuum in the scholarly community. The launch of the new blacklist by Cabells International, a scholarly analytics company in the US, several months later came at a perfect time and immediately attracted attention on social media and among those who have concerns over predatory publishing. People have wondered if the Cabells's blacklist is an extended service to Beall's venture (e.g., Forrester *et al.*, 2017), given that both have the same goals and efforts, and Beall was consulted at an early stage of the project. Cabells insists that its product is independently developed and makes great improvements upon Beall's blacklist, especially in its increased transparency and unbiased process, although they do take many titles from Beall's archive (Teixeira da Silva, 2020). They point to several particularly notable changes: (i) providing specific reasons and scores for each journal to be included, (ii) classifying violations into different levels of severity, i.e., from severe, to moderate, to minor, and (iii) developing a clear and fair appeals policy.

One of the concerns about Beall's criteria is their ambiguity in, or ignorance of, distinguishing a deceptive or fraudulent journal from an inexperienced but honest journal (Kendall, 2021). Cabells develops a journal scoring system to mediate. Basically, each identified behavioral indicator is assigned a score upon the severity of the offense, and all identified violations are categorized based on relative severity and subject matter. Under each category of severity, practices are examined in several areas. For example, the "severe" violations are reflected by the presence of certain attributes of a journal's practice in integrity, peer review, publication practices, indexing and metrics, and fees. For the "minor" violations, in addition to evaluating most of these areas, the characteristics of its website are taken into consideration. For example, if a web form is the only method for users to contact the journal, it is considered a minor violation, while if information received from the journal does not match the journal's own website, it is severe. Cabells forms a review board to analyze predatory behaviors and decide on the inclusion of predatory titles.

Cabells's Predatory Reports designated 65 behavioral indicators as its criteria in the beginning. Constant revisions to the criteria have resulted in 71 indicators in its Version 1.1 as of 2019 (Appendix B). Some indicators are more straightforward to analyze and execute than others. For example, one may wonder if Cabells really verifies with every editorial member of a journal when referring to this indicator: "the journal includes scholars on an editorial board without their knowledge or permission." Even if it does contact them, it is unknown if responses have always been received.

Studies have evaluated the reliability and usefulness of Cabells's blacklist. Among others, Dony *et al.* (2020) used an existing dataset of 10,123 journals (2012–2016) to test Cabells's coverage and methodology. The study reveals empty journals, questionable weighing, and a lack of rigor in how Cabells applies its own procedures. They also spot identical criteria being recorded multiple times against individual journal entries, and find some inconsistencies between reviewing dates and the criteria version. Two journals are found to be blacklisted twice with a different number of violations. Another study by Chen (2019) compared Beall's and Cabells's blacklists, and suggested that the former is more inclusive or aggressive and the latter is more conservative or careful.

Others tend to praise Cabells's contributions against deceptive and dishonest publications and its efforts to delineate low-quality journals (e.g., Anderson, 2017, 2019a). Cabells's effort is applauded for maintaining an authoritative source to help regulate scholarly publishing. Thus, although issues do exist in the criteria and in its implementation of the criteria, Cabells's journal blacklist is considered "a carefully crafted, honestly managed, and highly useful tool" (Anderson, 2019a).

Cabells's blacklist is presented as a searchable database with relevant services attached. A search function is provided for users to find a particular journal. In addition to its searchability, Cabells encourages users to suggest possible predatory publications and provides opportunities for journals to appeal against their inclusion. New titles suggested by users or identified through other channels are stored in a temporary review file awaiting evaluations by Cabells's review board and becomes viewable and downloadable by users.

The numbers of the journal entries in Table 3.2 illustrate the growth of Cabells's blacklist over time. Although the rate is not as fast as described by Bisaccio (2018) with 800–1,000 new titles added every month, there is indeed a steady increase within the timespan of three years. Cabells also keeps refining its selection criteria and improving its services by fixing existing problems and adding new features (Anderson, 2019a).

Unlike Beall's blacklists, Cabells's journal blacklist is subscription-based, alongside its other products and services: namely, its whitelist and author services. Pricing changes upon the size of the institution and history of the subscription. With subscriptions from over 750 universities worldwide (it is unknown if they all subscribe to the blacklist), Cabells's list is far from capable of serving the academic community. Scholars at small-sized, or even mid-sized, institutions have been largely left behind the paywall – let alone those affiliated with other types of organizations, and those from developing countries who cannot afford the subscription but are from the areas most targeted by predatory practices. Cabells's blacklist, though with improvements, is prevented by its subscription price from gaining the momentum of Beall's journal blacklist, at least in its current operation.

Table 3.2 Numbers of journals on Cabells's blacklist by year

Journal	Year	Month	Source
4,000	2017	Jun	Prasad, 2017
8,300	2018	Mar	Bisaccio, 2018
10,498	2019	Jan	Chen, 2019
11,839	2019	Aug	Dony et al., 2020
12,000	2019	Oct	Linacre, 2019
13,000	2020	Feb	Linacre, 2020

3.2.3 In-house blacklists

With Beall's standalone journal list no longer active and Cabells's blacklist not freely accessible, the academic community feels the need for a tool to help them avoid predatory publishing. Some institutions decide to create their own blacklists to regulate their tenure, promotion, and reappointment assessments. Such an institution-based list is more a binding promise between the organization and its employees than merely a suggestion. Authors tend to comply with their institutional policies more than listening to the warning of a third-party product.

Several institutional journal blacklists are reported in China (Cyranoski, 2018; Xu *et al.*, 2020), such as the list provided by Zhongshan Ophthalmic Center at Sun Yat-sen of journals labelled "controversial in the community," and the Obstetrics and Gynecology Hospital of Fudan University that creates its own list. Huaqiao University has its own blacklist that shows journals with heavy self-citing rates. The university asks its faculty to avoid these journals and warns that whoever publishes in the listed journals will be disciplined. Another institutional blacklist created by East China University of Political Science and Law (ECUPSL) in 2018 consists of 67 entries of social science journals published in the Chinese language.

As a specialized institution, it is relatively straightforward for ECUPSL to develop a group of titles, particularly when the focus is on the local language. But it remains controversial regarding the criteria for journal selections. The institution takes the following when measuring predatory journals: (i) those with 100+ papers per issue, (ii) those with multiple versions of one issue, e.g., academic, public, online, and mass media version, and (iii) those with various publishing frequencies for the same title, such as weekly, semi-monthly, etc. versions. These measures may be oversimplistic, but they look practicable for evaluation of journals in the relevant academic fields. Such institutional efforts seem effective for handling fraudulent practices and may represent an appropriate direction for the future combat with predatory publishing.

3.3 Whitelists of open access journals

If a blacklist is to help identify predatory publications, a whitelist is one that aims to present an index of vetted, presumably legitimate outlets. Many reputable scholarly indexes may serve as whitelists to check against when needing to verify the prestige of a journal. For example, the Web of Science (WoS) is a globally recognized index, and Medline and PubMed Central are famous in biomedical and life sciences as discipline-bound databases of electronic scholarly materials. However, these indexes are not designed to be OA journal whitelists with the purpose of battling predatory practices.

3.3.1 The Directory of Open Access Journals (DOAJ)

The most popular whitelist of OA journals is DOAJ. It was created in 2003 by Sweden's Lund University Libraries as a response to the discussion of OA scholarly publishing at the Nordic Conference on Scholarly Communication in 2002 (Hedlund & Rabow, 2009). It is designed to locate and access OA journals that are quality-controlled through peer review or editorial control by a minimum of two experts. Ten years later, the Infrastructure Services for Open Access, a non-profit organization, in the U.K. took over its operations.

The DOAJ is a community-curated online index (Olijhoek et al., 2015). Its operations are supported by (i) the DOAJ team of members from around the world, (ii) its advisory board and council that provide advice and recommendations to the DOAJ team, and (iii) its editorial subcommittee that provides advice and guidance to the managing editors. A group of more than 100 voluntary editorial staff reviews applications submitted by OA journals for inclusion. The management team makes sure that the volunteers do not have any conflicts of interest to guarantee fair reviews. The volunteers also include DOAJ's global ambassadors who are spread across the world to promote OA publishing.

For a journal to be included, its publisher will need to provide necessary information about the journal by filling out a DOAJ online application. An editor will evaluate the application by applying some basic criteria that ask the journal to be open access, actively publish scholarly work, and target researchers or practitioners as its readership. The editor will check the journal's website to make sure the information submitted is reliable and meets the professional standard of scholarly publishing. The editor may contact the publisher for more information during the review process.

When DOAJ was launched in 2003, it curated about 300 OA journals. By the end of 2020, this number climbed to more than 15,000 titles (Figure 3.2). Developed as a whitelist, it is expected to contain exclusively non-predatory journals. Yet a simple comparison between this list and Beall's blacklist reveals that "one in five of Beall's 'predatory' publishers had managed to get at least one of their journals into the DOAJ" (Bohannon, 2013, p. 62). Moreover, when Bohannon conducted his sting operation, he was surprised to find that up to 45% of the DOAJ publishers accepted his nonsense paper.

The DOAJ launched a re-application project in early 2015 by implementing more restrictive criteria with careful audits in order to verify its

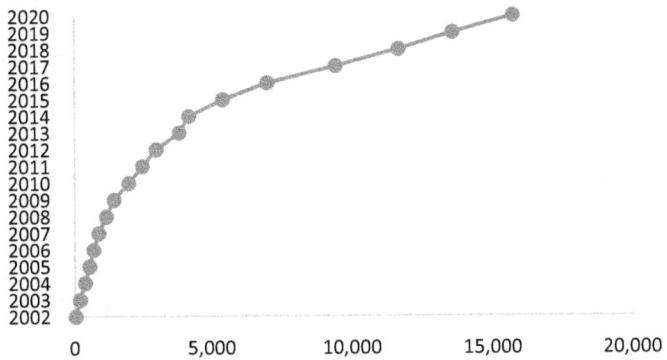

Figure 3.2 Increase of journals in DOAJ by year
Source: doaj.org

coverage. The project was finished in 2017, with more than 40% of the journals having been weeded out. Although it may have overreacted to Bohannon's operation (Sun, 2019), its newly implemented stringent criteria have indeed resulted in a clear quality improvement of the list (Marchitelli et al., 2017).

English is the language of publishing for 76% of DOAJ's journals. As many as 80 different languages are represented in the database. Figure 3.3 displays the top ten languages with their total number of journals as of early 2021. Regarding the geographic location of the publishers that publish DAOJ's journals, a total of 100 countries are represented. Figure 3.4 shows the top ten countries.

As a whitelist to collect accreditable OA journals, DOAJ's operations are transparent, and its dataset is freely available on the website. Financially, it is fully supported by donations through academic organizations and sponsors around the world; journals do not need to make a donation to be included. To use this site, a search box is designed to look for journal information from over 16,000 journals, as well as individual articles from more than 6,000,000 articles, as of spring 2021.

A certification is awarded to OA journals that exhibit best practices and achieve a high level of openness and publishing standards. Known as the DOAJ Seal, it requires journals to meet seven criteria to receive the award. The criteria measure journals on their establishment of the provenance, ownership, and editorial quality; facilitation of accessibility, sharing and discoverability; and efforts to provide the permanence of the publications through archiving and preservation requirements. The seal is not a

22 *Journals*

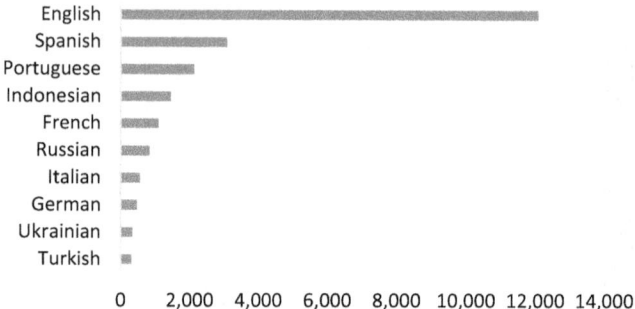

Figure 3.3 Top ten languages used by DOAJ journals
Source: doaj.org

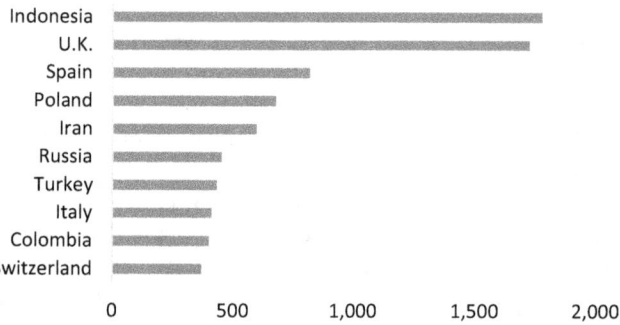

Figure 3.4 Top ten countries where DOAJ journals are published
Source: doaj.org

permanent award; failure to maintain best practices and standards may lead to removal of the seal. Around 10% of journals indexed in the DOAJ have been awarded the seal.

3.3.2 Cabells's whitelist

Long before Cabells started its blacklist, it managed an index of vetted business journals that was gradually developed into a full directory, known as Journalytics, with analytics and author services on established scholarly journals. As of early 2021, the whitelist contained more than 11,000 titles covering 18 academic disciplines for researchers and institutions to identify publishing opportunities.

Cabells maintains the Journalytics selection criteria to select journals that are based on invitations. The criteria are administered by a review board that evaluates certain areas of a journal's operations, including audience, relevance, sponsorship, quality, peer review, peers, policies, publication practices, and integrity. The review board may ask journals to provide additional information at any time, including original manuscripts and peer review comments on articles published in the journals. An annual audit on all journals is taken to monitor journal performance and delete those that no longer meet the criteria.

Journals in Cabells's whitelist are ranked and displayed on a "journal card" with important information about the journal. What are unique to the scorecards are the acceptance rate of submissions, types of peer review such as blind and double-blind, and the availability of peer review notes. There are three distinct indicators on the card: the Cabells Classification Index (CCI), the Difficulty of Acceptance metrics, and the median frequency of mention of articles from a particular journal in social media (Blobaum, 2018). CCI offers the normalized ranking of a journal within Cabells's subject categories to indicate the academic position of the journal in comparison to other journals in the same category. The Difficulty of Acceptance is assessed objectively by using institutional affiliation of the authors to calculate how often submissions are accepted, as Cabells believes that journals have higher levels of difficulty of acceptance if they tend to publish papers from high-performing institutions. Regarding the frequency of mentioning of articles on social media, Cabells converts article-level metrics into journal-level metrics.

Cabells does not make its application of the inclusion criteria transparent enough because its services are subscription-based. For example, the data for the citation ages and social media mentions is invisible, leaving readers wondering how to verify the results (Blobaum, 2018, p. 23). Also, some information used to calculate Cabells's metrics are out of date or inaccurate, notably the information about the levels of institutions' performance.

The questions in their proprietary metrics, their non-comprehensive coverage of legitimate titles, their relatively expensive subscription charge, and their inclusion of non-OA journals have limited their reach to the broader academic community as a useful whitelist (Colvin & Vinyard, 2016; Walters, 2016). Still, Cabells's whitelist is an alternative to the DOAJ for scholars to find proper publishing outlets and for librarians and information professionals to help others achieve their publishing goals.

3.3.3 In-house whitelists

In-house whitelists serve as guidelines for researchers to find acceptable publishing venues. Unlike generally designed whitelists such as the DOAJ list, in-house whitelists are more like a contract for employees or customers to follow, therefore serving as a stronger and more powerful tool to battle predatory publishing, especially if the lists are expressed as mandates.

a) The University Grants Commission's CARE list in India

As the only grant-giving agency managed by the Indian government, the University Grants Commission (UGC) requires grant seekers to publish in the journals on its CARE list. UGC also determines and maintains the professional standards in institutions of higher education, including the standards of teaching, examination, and research in universities, which makes its journal whitelist functional beyond grant seeking. According to the UGC, its CARE program is charged to identify, regularly audit, report, and maintain the UGC-CARE reference list of quality journals. The intent is to create a whitelist to respond to the extensive practices of predatory publishing in India and create awareness of academic integrity and publication ethics among researchers. The current list is a revised version of the early Approved List of Journals that suffered from flawed criteria and improper implementation (Tao, 2020). The revision withdrew around 3,000 entries from the original 5,000 journals to form its newest version in 2019.

Unfortunately, the UGC-CARE whitelist itself has been taken advantage of by some local publishers to promote their own businesses. Upon inclusion in the list, some journals "start behaving in predatory manner and try to lure authors by aggressively advertising their listing in UGC-CARE" (Tao, 2020). Such unexpected practices push the UGC to update its list every quarter to keep up its quality and integrity. In addition, the CARE site does not release its journal inclusion criteria, making judgments of the quality of its journal selections difficult.

b) Disciplinary whitelists

The merit of disciplinary whitelists is that the creators are experts in their own fields and capable of compiling reliable scholarly sources. Institutions may adopt the lists in relevant disciplines once they have been proven to be trustworthy. An ideal strategy to combat predatory publishing is that policymakers and seasoned scholars across the world, or across regions within a country if language becomes a concern, collaborate to develop whitelists for as many academic disciplines as possible.

The Journal Quality List (JQL) established by the Australian Business Deans Council (ABDC) is an example of recognized disciplinary whitelists for all fields of business management. Initiated in 2007, the ABDC created a journal list to help guide researchers in the selection of quality outlets. Its 2010 version contains 2,671 journal entries covering statistics and other business management. There have been some revisions since then, but the total number of journals has remained relatively constant (ABDC, 2019).

Expert panels are selected to represent each discipline and are responsible for creating and reviewing the JQL in accordance with detailed Terms of Reference approved by the ABDC. An online submission form is designed to receive recommendations and input from people. For journals to be included, a set of criteria are verified which emphasize peer review quality. Journals are ranked into A*, A, B, and C categories based on renowned journal metrics such as WoS and the evaluation of each journal on its quality and relevance indicators. The 2019 version of the JQL endorses 2,682 journal entries, falling in the following groups (Table 3.3):

Table 3.3 Journal ranks in JQL (source: ABDC, 2019)

Rank	# Journals	Percent
Journals A*	199	7.41%
Journals A	651	24.27%
Journals B	850	31.69%
Journals C	982	36.61%

The ABDC provides appropriate levels of administrative support to the expert panels by organizing a steering group to conduct a final review of the list. Before each final review, the ABDC usually invites feedback from key stakeholders, including the panel and steering group members, as well as ABDC members, the academy, and publishers. For over a decade, JQL has been used not only by institutions of higher education in Australia, but has also been adopted by business programs at universities in other countries; for example, JQL has been adopted by the business school at Thompson Rivers University in Canada as its *de facto* journal ranking authority (Pyne, 2017).

There is another Journal Quality List with a similar purpose, created by Anne-Wil Harzing in 2002 at Bradford University (harzing.com). There are also several other comprehensive lists of academic journals in the fields of business management, such as the Academic Journal Guide by the Chartered Association of Business Schools and the Erasmus Research Institute of Management Journals List. They are all available online as alternatives, free of charge to download.

Another example is the International Academy of Nursing Editors, which collaborates with the *Nurse Author & Editor* journal to create the Directory of Nursing Journals for journals. It is professionally evaluated and vetted within the nursing community (Thorne *et al.*, 2014). Authors in the field of nursing are encouraged to remain vigilant against the penetration of predatory publishing and to check the directory before submitting papers for publication.

3.3.4 Crowd-sourced services

Many independent projects have created web tools to assist authors in the identification of trusted OA journals. They use crowdsourcing to engage the academic community in the ranking of a large quantity of journals by inviting individuals to contribute to journal scoring (van Gerestein, 2015). There is a long list of such services (see Table 3.4), but all are at an early stage of development and struggle with obtaining enough users' input (Perkel, 2015).

3.4 Comparison of blacklists and whitelists

Strinzel *et al.* (2019) carried out a systematic analysis of the criteria used by selected blacklists and whitelists. Applying both quantitative and qualitative methods, they probe differences in the criteria for quality. Focusing on the same subject but using a distinct approach, Cobey *et al.* (2018) took a

Table 3.4 A selected list of crowd-sourced services

Service	Creation	Character
Quality Open Access Market	Radboud Univ. Netherlands	Encourages scholars to score journals & share experience about journals to match publishing service against price
JournalGuide	North Carolina, US	Collects data from industry, public domains, and individual scholars to rank & assess publications
SciRev	Researchers for Researchers	Finds journals with short waiting times by emphasizing review and publishing process
Edanz Journal Selector	Japan	Partners with major publishers to support non-English speakers in journal selections, offers fee-based editing and reviewing services

scoping review to summarize the epidemiological characteristics of selection criteria for predatory journals and pointed to the need to develop a standardized definition for identifying predatory journals.

A comparison of journal inclusions between Beall's and Cabells's blacklists, and DOAJ and Cabells's whitelists, reveals heavy overlap between the two blacklists (see Figure 3.5). This implies that when the Cabells developed its blacklist, it may have used Beall's collection as a source of entries. The overlaps between the two whitelists are also large in the absolute total, although Strinzel et al. (2019) describe it as a "relatively small overlap." Even counting its smaller ratio in comparison to the ratio of overlaps between the blacklists, the whitelist overlaps are sizable, particularly with the fact that OA journals are only part of the Cabells's whitelist while the DOAJ list contains exclusively OA journals. This may indicate that the two whitelists have developed similar criteria for journal inclusions.

Strinzel et al. (2019) suggest "false positives" and "false negatives" in the identification of predatory journals. In other words, new and inexperienced journals may be mistakenly labelled as fraudulent on the blacklists, or dubious journals may be tagged as acceptable publications on the whitelists. Another possibility is the existence of a gray area in predatory journal classification caused by likely ambiguous criteria, or due to changes in publishing practices of some journals. The discussion of "false positives" and "false negatives" is expanded by Teixeira de Silva and Tsigaris (2018) who theorize common mistakes made in any selection process.

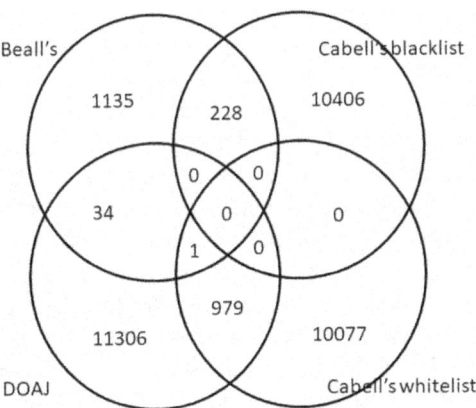

Figure 3.5 Journal overlaps between selected blacklists and whitelists
Source: Strinzel et al., 2019, FIG 1

Both Cobey *et al.* and Strinzel *et al.* believe that the blacklists' criteria focus more on a journal's business operations, e.g., the editorial services and publishing practices, than on its scholarly quality. In contrast, whitelists pay more attention to policy, peer review, and editorial services. In logistical terms, a whitelist is easier to identify, update, and manage. It does not need to constantly track down new predatory journals. Instead, the burden is on the journals to validate themselves (Nature Editorial, 2018). For an author, it is also more straightforward to follow the suggestions of a whitelist than to filter out titles on a blacklist when attempting to find the appropriate publishing opportunities. None of the existing blacklists is an exclusive list of problematic journals; thus, one may end up publishing in a predatory journal that has not yet been listed on the blacklists. Although one may argue that none of the existing whitelists is a perfect list, the DOAJ has been overwhelmingly trusted.

Strong criticism of both the blacklists and whitelists comes from Teixeira da Silva and co-authors (e.g., Teixeira da Silva, 2013, 2017; Teixeira da Silva & Tsigaris, 2018), who believe that none of these sources is reliable in the selection of OA publishing outlets. They consider Beall's blacklists as the "original sin" that causes an unfair delisting of some valid OA journals by the DOAJ and the Cabells's whitelists. Similarly, the Cabells's blacklist inherits unfortunate weaknesses from the criteria and content of Beall's standalone journal blacklist. They think that Beall's blacklist is deeply flawed due to his hard-to-measure selection standards, his murky applications of the criteria, and his negative attitude toward OA. They blame the whitelists and blacklists for having contaminated the ecosystem of OA publishing, because when a whitelist is developed, existing blacklists are referenced, and vice versa.

Beyond blacklists and whitelists, there is a gray OA journal concept created and advocated by Walt Crawford (2017a). His aim is to amend Beall's work on blacklists. He defines gray OA as "gold OA journals that are not in DOAJ" (Crawford, 2017a, p. 1). The gray OA list will include both non-predatory and predatory journals, since there are journals that do not fit into the category of predatory journals, but have not applied for registration in the DOAJ. When Crawford describes his method of data collection for the "Gray OA Universe" (pp. 2–3), he seems to have used Beall's two blacklists exclusively. The steps of his data collection include: (i) copying and examining Beall's journal list against the DOAJ to remove duplicates, (ii) using Beall's publisher blacklist to find journals not present on the standalone journal list, (iii) collecting journals' demographics for his reports in his own publication *Cites and Insights*, and (iv) removing titles from the list that also appear in the DOAJ. It becomes clear that the gray journal list is actually a blacklist and limited only to Beall's coverage, unless Crawford has published additional work on the gray OA list that the author is unaware of.

3.5 Some characteristics of predatory journals

Predatory journals have introduced multiple forms of unprofessional and unethical practices, such as the 109 unique characteristics by Cobey et al. (2018). Because of the space limit, the following descriptions highlight only the major practices of predatory publishing.

3.5.1 Volume of predatory publications

The condition of predatory publishing is primarily represented by the volume of publications, e.g., how many articles published in predatory journals and how many journals identified as predatory. The most thorough exploration of such numbers is taken by Crawford (2017a, 2017b) and Björk and colleagues (e.g., Björk et al., 2020; Shen & Björk, 2015). The latter studies calculate the volumes by applying the stratified random sampling method, while the former manually check the websites of most predatory journals and publishers. Crawford's numbers are broken into strata or granular categories, making it possible to look into many aspects of predatory practices. Many of the descriptions below cite Crawford's data unless mentioned otherwise.

Predatory journals started around 2006–2007, though there were a few attempts beforehand. Within several years, the number of predatory journals climbed steeply to their peak in 2013–2014. Since then, the total number experienced a slight decline until its rebound in 2017–2018. The recorded numbers of predatory journals were 7,743 in 2015 (including 5,988 active ones) and 7,860 in 2017 (Crawford, 2017a, 2017b). Björk et al. (2020) adjusted the number to more than 10,000 journals in 2018.

For the total number of articles in predatory journals, Shen and Björk (2015) reported 420,000 in 2014, while Crawford (2017a) counted 255,183 for the same year. This difference reflects confusing practices of predatory publishing, e.g., some journals are created but never publish any articles, some publish very few articles, and some fluctuate their article numbers from year to year or even from issue to issue. In 2014 alone, a high of 23% of predatory journals did not publish any articles, even though they had in previous years. In general, the numbers of predatory journals and papers are undoubtedly vast enough to do damage to the scholarly publishing enterprise.

Mega-journals are unique to OA publishing and noticeable in predatory publishing. For example, two predatory journals were found to produce

30 Journals

Table 3.5 Size of journals and their total number of articles in 2015

Articles per journal	Total journals	Total articles
97+	752 (13%)	206,959 (70%)
50–96	745 (12%)	38,291 (13%)
31–49	699 (12%)	19,503* (6%)
10–30	2,050 (34%)	25,590 (9%)
1–9	1,742 (29%)	6,620 (2%)
Total	5,988	296,963

Source: Crawford, 2017a, Tables 5.1 & 5.2. * indicates a miscount

Table 3.6 Numbers and percentages of predatory journals and articles by segment in 2015

	HSS	Biomed	STEM	Total
Journal	1,269 (24%)	1,816 (35%)	2,167 (41%)	5,252
Article	9,1750 (35%)	6,2818 (24%)	10,7830 (41%)	262,398

Source: Crawford, 2017a, Table 5.5

over 4,000 articles during their peak from 2012–2016; one published more than 3,000 articles, and eleven journals each published more than 2,000 articles. Altogether, 13% of journals, each having 97+ articles, published 70% of all predatory articles in 2015 (Table 3.5). In contrast, the predatory market has been filled mostly by journals publishing fewer than 30 articles per year. A high of 34% of predatory journals each publish 10–30 articles, followed by 29% of journals that publish only 1–9 articles each.

One large difference between predatory and legitimate journals is their subject coverage. In order to attract as many submissions as possible to boost profits, most predatory journals set a broad scope. For example, a journal may take research in all social science fields, plus all subjects in the humanities, etc. According to Crawford (2017a), roughly three broad segments of academic disciplines comprised most predatory publications in 2015 (Table 3.6). While STEM studies dominate these journals and articles, a smaller number of the humanities and social science journals (24%) provide more articles (35%), in contrast to biomedical publications that have 35% of journals but produce only 24% of all articles.

3.5.2 Article processing charges

Many non-predatory OA journals also take APCs to support their operations and permit them to offer free access (Björk & Solomon, 2014). Thus, requiring APCs is not necessarily an exclusive sign of predatory publishing, although almost all predatory journals require an APC. The difference between predatory journals and other OA journals in asking for APCs is whether APCs are taken for the sole purpose of making a profit. Such a judgment needs to be made together with an analysis of other characteristics, e.g., the existence of low-quality content, cheating practices in operations, and lack of editorial and publishing services.

Early in predatory publishing, journals tended to hide information about APCs, resulting in an unpleasant surprise for authors who received a bill without knowing about it in advance. It created tremendous tension between publishers and authors, and ended up with many authors refusing to pay such fees. Gradually, more journals changed their practice and posted fee requirements on their websites. Crawford (2017a) found about 12% of predatory journals did not release APC information in 2015; this percentage was reduced to 8.6% two years later (Crawford, 2017b).

Many journals set two rates of APCs because they are created and operated in developing countries: one rate for local authors, and the other for international authors. Discount rates for students, low-income groups, and the like are set, but this is not a common practice. Both the local currency and US dollar are typically accepted. The Indian rupee is the most popular currency, followed by US dollar, Euro, and British pound. Most standalone journals set a low APC rate, mainly under $50 USD. Table 3.7 shows statistics for a group of 318 predatory journals surveyed in early 2014.

In another study, Xia (2014a) examined two Indian mega-journals and found that their APCs are INR 1,500–3,000, which is around 5% of a lower-middle-class household's monthly average income in India. Calculating APCs for one of the mega-journals, it was found that the journal could gain an annual revenue of INR 6,030,000 = 2,010 (number of articles) × 3,000 (APC per article). As a comparison, the annual income range of a lower-middle-class Indian household in 2013 was INR 200,000–500,000 (Meyer & Birdsall, 2013). If this is a single-publisher operated journal, as defined by Beall's standalone journals, this publisher could enjoy a decent

Table 3.7 APC rates in US dollars

	Journals also charging rupee	*All journals charging APCs*
Mean	$37	$94
Median	$32	$51
Minimum	$8	$8
Maximum	$96	$950

Source: Xia, 2014b, Table 1

life by investing in this business venture. Thus, there is a large incentive for the publisher to expand the capability of the journal by accepting all submissions without performing quality control. This is the exact motive for opportunists to launch predatory publishing business in the first place.

3.5.3 Scholarly quality

A journal's content is its primary indicator of scholarly quality. However, this is a highly subjective measure because it requires an individual's judgment. Two experts may offer totally conflicting opinions on the same product. Although this does not necessarily prevent one from applying other, more objective measures, such measures tend to be indirect, labor-intensive, and only suggestive. It explains why there are relatively few efforts to conduct such identifications of predatory publications.

One quantitative measure of quality is the analysis of citation types and numbers. Citations represent recognition that publications being cited have academic value. Citation of predatory journals has been explored by several studies, each of which observes low citation counts. For example, Björk et al. (2020) found 67% of predatory articles in their samples do not receive any citations at all. In another study of seven possible predatory journals (Anderson, 2019b), it was discovered that five receive very few citations, while two do not receive any citations. Predatory journals have been largely ignored by the academic community. Detailed discussion is available in Chapter 5.

A direct measure of quality was taken to check language use and plagiarism (Xia, 2014a). By randomly selecting two journals from Beall's blacklist, the study found that more than half of their articles contain obvious grammatical and language problems. A few, although not many, articles publish more than once across journals or even in the same journal. Many articles have confusing ordering and formatting of their citation-reference items.

In addition to the cosmetic check, another study took larger samples and focused on the evaluation of scholarly quality for selected predatory publications on their methodological designs and research protocols (Moher et al., 2017). After examining thousands of predatory journals, it found that the articles typically miss critical information necessary for readers to evaluate and reproduce the findings. Biomedical studies regularly apply randomized trials to separate treatment groups from control groups in order to avoid bias and make comparisons. However, in the samples, only fewer than 10% of studies described registration of randomized controlled trials, and fewer than one quarter mentioned the double-blind method. Even among those that did describe randomized controlled trials, fewer than 14%

provided a registration number or registry name. Moreover, only 40% of the articles mentioned approvals by an ethics committee when humans or animals are involved, which is the standard of mainstream studies. The study paid special attention to the waste of money, since many of the published projects are sponsored by major funders such as the US National Institutes of Health: "at least 18,000 funded biomedical-research studies are tucked away in poorly indexed, scientifically questionable journals" (Moher et al., 2017, p. 24).

Using an automated language analysis technique, Markowitz et al. (2014) studied whether predatory journals differ from legitimate journals in their writing styles. They analyzed and judged word types to examine the role of language in understanding truthful and dishonest discourse patterns. By comparing two groups of journals, i.e., predatory journals from Beall's blacklist and reputable journals from WoS, the study checked the writing styles in the About Us and Aim/Scope sections on their websites and found that language in predatory journals does favor more discrepancy words (e.g., "would") and positive emotions to promote their publications and attract authors and users. As a comparison, reputable journals use more functional terms and more propositions (e.g., "in") and take more quantifiers (e.g., "more") as well as words related to causality. It concluded that observable patterns of different writing styles do exist between the two types of publishing practices, and identifying these patterns may potentially assist in the assessment of predatory versus legitimate journals.

3.5.4 Cheating behaviors

Cheating has been widely detected in predatory publishing, where false information is aptly engineered and deliberately provided to take advantage of researchers' unawareness of scholarly misconduct and eagerness to publish. Hiding APCs is one form of cheating, and providing an inaccurate location of a publisher's operations is another. In the latter scenario, a publisher pretends to be in a developed country, usually the US, while the actual operations are in a developing country. It is an attempt to make a journal look more attractive, because publishing in a Western-based journal provides more career merit. Predatory journals also forge their titles and frequently name themselves things like *American Journal of* . . . , *Canadian Journal of* . . . , *British Journal of* . . ., etc. while the journals may have no connections at all to the mentioned countries. Many journals also choose titles like *International Journal of* . . . , *Global Journal of* . . . , *World Journal of* . . . , and claim that their journals are leading scholarly journals in the world, when in fact they are brand new and struggling with an adequate number of submissions. Crawford (2017a, p. 66) found 3,277 journals out of his recorded 18,910 journals begin with "International Journal" in their titles (17%). Of the 10,019 empty journals from 2012–2016, about 67% have a title beginning with the following common prefixes (Table 3.8):

Table 3.8 Common prefixes of predatory journal titles

Journal prefix	# Journals	% Journals
Universal Open...	1,215	12.13%
International Journal...	1,002	10.00%
Asian American...	742	4.71%
British Open...	681	6.80%
European Open...	534	5.33%
Eurasian...	529	5.28%
North American Open...	527	5.26%
Academic Open...	520	5.19%
US Open...	450	4.49%
Canadian Open...	430	4.29%
American Open...	351	3.50%

Source: Crawford, 2017a

False information on the websites of most predatory journals is presented in many other forms as well, including (i) erroneously claiming to carry out peer review while accepting all submissions, (ii) listing indexing databases that either themselves are predatory in nature or have never actually indexed the journals, (iii) citing artificial journal impact factor (JIF) scores that resemble the prestigious WoS JIF, e.g., Universal Impact Factor, Global Impact Factor, etc., (iv) claiming to collaborate with renowned academic organizations but the relationship is nonexistent, (v) forcibly listing scholars as their editors or editorial board members without their consent, and so on. Many of these forms of cheating are discussed in the following chapters.

3.5.5 Longevity

From the beginning, predatory publishing has presented a volatile market. Due to the low threshold of investment and high competition for submissions, journals come and go easily. Making a profit is the only purpose of these journals; as a result, publishers will quickly give up when a journal does not have enough papers to publish. Data shows that many journals, at any given time, have published very few, or even zero, articles. For example, Crawford (2017a) counted 350 journals that have not published any content since 2013, and 549 journals that have not published since 2014. He found the total number of empty journals during 2012–2016 to be as large as 10,019 titles. In addition, there are more journals that publish only

Table 3.9 Numbers of journals disappeared by year

# Journals	Year
661	2012
514	2013
402	2014
502	2015

Source: Crawford, 2017a

a couple of articles annually. Studies of predatory journals pay more attention to those with content than those without, because the latter provide less information on their dying websites. Each year, alongside the creation of numerous new predatory journals, there are a number of existing journals which evaporate or merge. Crawford (2017a) provided the following numbers of dead journals for each year (Table 3.9).

It will be a disaster for authors when a journal with scholarly content goes away. Predatory journals are extensively unwilling to invest on archiving capabilities, such as archiving their content on third-party websites. These short-lived journals, when in operation, do not offer transparent information about their content archiving polices. Once they go offline, articles published there will become unavailable immediately and permanently. Fortunately, the impact on science is minimal, because an overwhelming number of these articles have barely any scientific impact and have never been cited by other publications.

3.6 Tips on avoiding predatory journals

3.6.1 Innocent victims

The publishing market is murky for researchers who need to publish, but who feel confused and overwhelmed in choosing appropriate locations. Some know that their research cannot be published in WoS-indexed journals, or do not have time for a long review process by legitimate journals. They may be aware of predatory publishing, but do not have access to a trusted blacklist. They might benefit from consulting whitelists, but they may not know the lists exist, are clueless about how to use them, do not trust them, and so on. Researchers in some countries face the dilemma of combing through too much confusing information, while researchers in other countries have very limited access to adequate information due to technological deficiencies, language barriers, etc. Proper guidance will help them achieve their publishing goals.

The first step is to avoid email invitations. Studies have extensively pointed to template-like spam emails that have grammatical errors and cover a broad range of academic subjects. However, there are cases where emails are sent to researchers in the right fields without obvious language problems (e.g., Cobey et al., 2018). The rule of thumb is to ignore all of them because established journals rarely invite scholars, especially junior scholars, for submissions. Even if a few invitations are legitimate, one ought not take the risk unless the inviting journals are known sources.

The second option is to follow a whitelist. This is the optimal choice if a researcher's institution maintains a list of acceptable journals, or if there is a subject-based list of reliable journals such as the Journal Quality List by the ABDC in business management. When such a list is not available, DOAJ is a good alternative. Searching DOAJ by subject will result in a group of OA journals in a particular field. All journals are stewarded by DOAJ editors, reviewed by peers, and published in different languages. Many may not be as eminent in scholarly reputation as those on the WoS list, but are still academically acceptable, which suits the needs of authors whose articles cannot meet the standard of WoS journals.

A recently designed platform, Think.Check.Submit, is exactly the tool to help users identify trusted journals and publishers. It consolidates various information and practical resources to "educate researchers, promote integrity, and build trust in credible research and publications." It does not provide any specific list of journals because it believes that such a list can become outdated frequently, and publishing standards vary by discipline. Instead, it instructs users in how to make good decisions whenever they seek to submit their work to journals. As such, the platform is mostly regarded as an educational campaign that empowers researchers to assess journals. Confidence to make a judgment about a journal or publisher is what many authors need, and this confidence can be gained through learning and practice.

The Think.Check.Submit initiative takes a neutral stance to avoid any subjective judgment on a journal. It provides a checklist of questions and trustworthy resources on the verification of industry standards as well as professional ethics. It is a cross-industry initiative created by many known organizations, e.g., the Committee on Publication Ethics (COPE) and the DOAJ, to combat predatory publishing. As of early 2021, it is available in 41 languages, providing it with a global scope.

Its "think" function lets users acquire materials useful to understand resources pertinent to academic publishing and access up-to-date guidance about publisher issues and practices. Its "check" function reminds users to verify the credentials of particular publishing venues through a variety of tools and by following clear suggestions. For example, users may be advised to check APC requirements, peer review, and other professional signs of a journal to confirm that the publisher belongs to known publishing initiatives such as COPE, the Open Access Scholarly Publishers' Association (OASPA), etc. Through its "submit" function, users can confirm that they have selected a proper publishing outlet upon completing the platform's checklist with correct answers.

3.6.2 Willing participants

There is an increasing number of authors who are aware that they have submitted to predatory journals (Bagues *et al.*, 2019; Pyne, 2017). Of the four reasons proposed by Kurt (2018) about why these authors choose to do so, three are pertinent: (i) feeling of an affinity to a particular group, (ii) high pressure, and (iii) lack of research proficiency.

For all three causes, a radical change of the local academic culture is required with joint efforts from all stakeholders. From a geopolitical perspective, decision-makers have an interest in creating an image of productive research output to showcase their country, region, or institution. Once they recognize the negative impact of predatory publishing on their image, they may be the first to change their policies. This is particularly visible in many developing countries that have started to create more stringent academic regulations, showing positive signs of possible cultural change. Policies have the power to reshape the publishing landscape and guide future developments in many areas. Promoting awareness among all stakeholders, particularly decision-makers, has been and will still be the best strategy to fight unethical practices and influence on policymaking.

No matter what reasons are behind researchers' knowing participation in predatory publishing, authors need to be conscious that such benefits are only temporary. In the long run, they will suffer from their actions after the predatory outlets have become well-known in the academic community. Damage to one's personal reputation is hardly reparable. Evidence shows that more than 70% of authors who have published in presumed predatory journals are not proud of their "achievements," and refuse to answer awareness-related questions, as shown in a recent survey on knowledge and motivations of predatory publishing (Cobey *et al.*, 2019). The decision to balance short-term and long-term goals is researchers' own.

3.7 Conclusion

This chapter highlights only the major characteristics of predatory journals. Others are either covered in the following chapters or too minor to address. There is a good deal of controversy in the discussion of predatory publishing, including the use of the term itself, its criteria, application of the criteria, and its consequences. This chapter focused on Beall's criteria and blacklists, as well as other major lists such as several journal whitelists, but the introduction is not exclusive. For instance, many journal-evaluation and journal-ranking tools, such as the Cristin system in Norway, the Publindex system in Colombia, and Excellence in Research Australia, are not widely used and are, therefore, not introduced here.

4 Publishers

This chapter focuses on some practices by predatory publishers that have not been discussed extensively in the previous chapter. It uses some examples to highlight the business models of the publishers, and describes major legal challenges against, and by, some publishers. At the end, efforts taken by a few countries to battle predatory publishing are outlined.

Single-journal publishers are not included in this chapter. Broadly defined, both of Beall's lists are the publisher blacklists. While one list contains the names of publishers that produce two or more journals, the standalone journal list can also be a blacklist of publishers, because journals on it are those created and operated by single-journal publishers. Since the previous chapter discussed standalone journals, this chapter focuses on the publisher list. Comparatively, the publisher blacklist is more heterogeneous in nature in terms of publishers' size, operating locations, and investment terms.

4.1 The development of the publisher blacklist

The birth of Jeffrey Beall's list of predatory publishers was roughly two years earlier than his list of standalone predatory journals. The former was created in 2010, which was then expanded into two lists, including the latter (Beall, 2013a). Figure 4.1 shows the quick growth of the publisher blacklist from its beginning to its end in early 2017. The number of publishers exceeded 100 in mid-2012, climbing to 1,000 in early 2016, and reaching 1,163 by the time the list was removed. If the numbers of the cloned Beall's lists are taken into account, this growth trend seems to continue.

Beall maintained his publisher blacklist and regularly added two blog posts per week to his website. In each post, he made updates by introducing new names, analyzing existing entries, and removing low-quality but honest titles (Figure 4.2). When the numbers increased rapidly, he changed the form of announcements and introduced only the most controversial or representative publishers.

DOI: 10.4324/9781003029335-4

40 *Publishers*

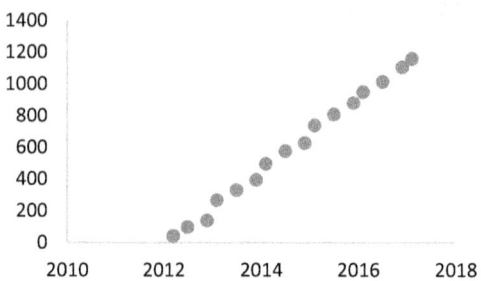

Figure 4.1 Increase of predatory publishers over time
Source: scholarlyoa.org

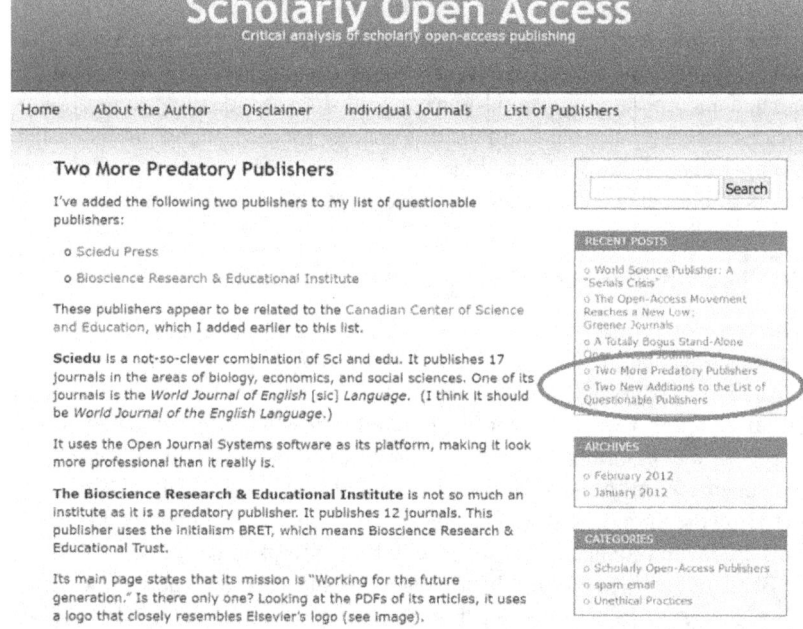

Figure 4.2 Screenshot of announcement for adding new publishers to the blacklist
Source: scholarlyoa.org, posted on 8 February 2012

In the development of the blacklist, misidentifications sometimes occurred, and changes were often needed due to new evidence. Hindawi, an open access (OA) commercial publisher of science, technology, and medicine literature, saw its name listed by Beall in 2010 because it was found to (i) send spam emails to solicit submissions, (ii) ask staff, rather than editors, to make publication decisions, (iii) recruit unusually large editorial boards, and (iv) publish with a very broad subject coverage (Beall, 2013b). Hindawi replied to Beall's criticism, presented its operations, and successfully convinced him to remove it from the list. Another example is the Multidisciplinary Digital Publishing Institute (MDPI), also an OA scholarly publisher, that was brought onto Beall's publisher blacklist in 2014 but was taken off upon a successful appeal by the company in 2015.

Beall provided an appeals system, which was proven to work well by the above cases. Figure 4.3 is a screenshot of the appeals page on scholarlyoa.org, showing the instructions for making a complaint to Beall and a four-member advisory board. The fact that few such appeals records have been reported indicates that most of the listed publishers have no intention of reforming their operations to meet professional standards. Making any changes requires investment, whereas making profit is the ultimate interest of all predatory publishers. It helps defend Beall against the criticism that his blacklist has jeopardized the chances of fresh and inexperienced publishers for improvement.

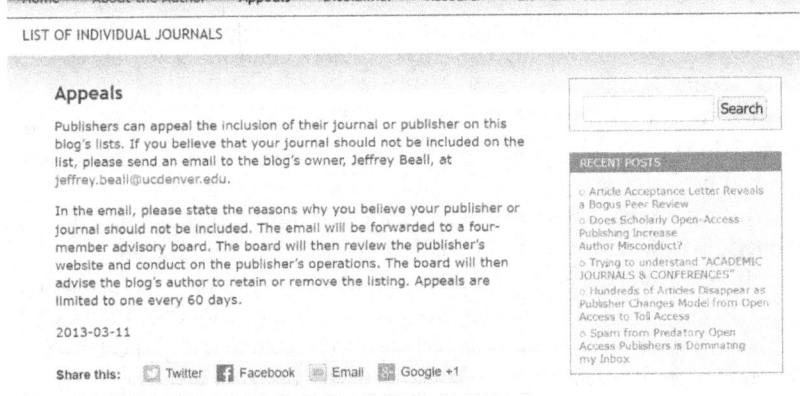

Figure 4.3 Screenshot of Beall's instructions for appeals
Source: scholarlyoa.org, posted on 11 March 2013

4.2 Predatory criteria revisited

The criteria developed by Beall include a checklist that applies to both predatory journals and publishers. A close look at the criteria reveals that the measures go back and forth between diagnosing journals and publishers. For example, within the same criteria, the measure of "publish a large fleet of journals" is for publishers, while "journal falsely claims impact factor" is more of a measure of journals (see Appendix A). All available criteria have the same purpose of identifying predatory behaviors in OA publishing, so separating journals from publishers in the criteria seems artificial and unnecessary.

To reiterate the discussion of the main characteristics of predatory publishing, a publisher is assessed as a predatory publisher when it (i) charges an article processing charge (APC) but does not provide necessary editorial or publishing services, (ii) fails to follow accepted standards or best practices in scholarly publishing, e.g., peer review, and (iii) engages in unethical practices, e.g., cheating in its operations. A publisher does not need to satisfy all of these criteria to be deemed predatory, nor has anyone set a threshold to quantify predatory behaviors.

It is not impossible for the same publisher to produce both predatory and non-predatory journals, depending on whether the publisher recruits serious scholars into its editorship and gives them the autonomy to make publishing decisions. The quality of publications under the same publisher can vary from journal to journal, if quality refers to citation status. But when predatory behaviors are considered, the co-existence is more hypothetical than real. There is a fundamental conflict between maximizing profit and controlling quality because the former relies on accepting as many submissions as possible, while the latter requires controlling the acceptance rate. Several conflicts between MDPI and its editors illustrate this type of tension (e.g., de Vrieze, 2018). There is no thorough discussion in the literature to explore this complexity and verify whether the combination does exist in practice.

This brings up another concern about defining predatory publishing: namely, whether there are various levels of severity in predatory behaviors by publishers, just as there are for journals, as described previously in Chapter 3 under Blacklists of Predatory Journals. The Cabells's journal blacklist has defined various levels of severity that may be applicable to the identification of predatory publishers, e.g., those that have never made any improvements since listed, those that have made only cosmetic changes, and those that have made real progress while still showing a minor level of predatory behaviors. Seeking profit is the interest of all commercial publishers, including legitimate ones, but smart publishers know that high quality is key to sustaining a long-term business. Although predatory publishers are after a different market, they will benefit from the same sustainable business rule: maintainable, supportive, and capable of holding up over time.

Unlike Beall's journal blacklist, which has been taken over by Cabells, his publisher list has become history and is only available through web archives. Though two anonymous groups in Europe have carried on Beall's endeavor in maintaining and updating publisher titles, their updates are minimal, and their cloned lists are no longer treated by the academic community as the go-to tools. It requires tremendous energy and time to detect and identify potential candidates, but most importantly, retaining a blacklist of OA publishers can be a dangerous job. In the worst-case scenario, it may bring in legal threats and cost the creator their job; at the very least, one will inevitably be assaulted and defamed, as Beall has experienced. It is safer to list an individual journal or single-journal publisher that does not have necessary resources to launch such attacks. Unless real efforts are resumed, future battles against predatory publishing will have to be taken on primarily at the level of journals.

4.3 Some practices by predatory publishers

4.3.1 Location of business operations

Although the previous chapter briefly discussed this practice, the descriptions here offer more details. There is a pattern in misinformation about publishers' locations: namely, many predatory publishers use an address in the West, preferably the US, Canada, Australia, or western European countries, while the operations are actually based in a developing nation. Such a Western address is commonly found to be fake, including (i) a residential address, e.g., an apartment number in London, (ii) a PO box in Delaware, (iii) a warehouse address in the middle of nowhere in Texas, (iv) an invalid address, or (v) any other types of nonsense address. Crawford (2017) estimated that "90% or more . . . listed as being published in the United States, United Kingdom or Canada are actually published elsewhere, based on the peculiar syntax of the webpages" (p. 40).

Google Maps can help locate the addresses. There are also many other ways to verify that the actual location of a publisher's operations may not be what it claims. Below is an incomplete list of verification methods.

1 The publisher is using a web form as its contact page, indicating that it does not intend to let authors and readers contact its listed address, which is presented only to falsify its location of operations.

2 The publisher is using a commercial email address, such as Gmail, Yahoo, or Hotmail, indicating that it attempts to save money in every area of its operations and avoid disclosing its geographic affiliation.
3 The publisher has a web domain in the location of a developing country, indicating that it relies on a local server.
4 The publisher has an IP address in a developing country, which provides more direct evidence.
5 The publisher asks for APCs with a currency other than the currency of the country where its address appears. In most cases, when local currency is charged, another Western currency such as the US dollar, English pound, or Euro is concurrently accepted.
6 The publisher targets authors in a specific location other than the country where it lists its address, which indicates its proximity to that location.
7 The publisher provides a bank account in a developing country for the purpose of collecting APCs, which is the strongest evidence of misrepresentation of the publisher's real location.

Many publishers do not provide an address. It was found that 28% of predatory publishers did not record a country of publication in 2015 (Crawford, 2017). For those that do provide the information, the misrepresentation of their locations makes the analysis of their geographic distributions unreliable. According to data, only a few countries dominate the global predatory publishing market (Table 4.1). However, it is obvious that the numbers for the US, Canada, and the UK are exaggerated.

Most studies find a pattern of predatory publishers being located in a few developing countries. In Bohannon's sting operation, about one-third of the

Table 4.1 Top ten countries with predatory publications in 2015

Country	Publications
India	161,920
US	17,442
Canada	7,892
UK	5,800
Pakistan	3,925
Nigeria	2,779
Bangladesh	2,613
Bulgaria	1,824
Romania	1,729
Singapore	1,389

Source: Crawford, 2017, Table 7.3

samples were based in India, where 81% of publishers accepted his flawed papers, making India "the world's largest base for open-access publishing" (Bohannon, 2013, p. 64). India has been consistently observed as the leading contributor to predatory publishing (Hegde & Patil, 2021). Beall (2012) detected new predatory publishers in India every week. Among many other studies of predatory publishers that have mentioned India, the following are listed to highlight their geographical spread:

1 Demir (2018) used predatory publishers' IP contact locations to identify 62% of them as being located in India. In comparison, only 48% of publishers self-identified as being in India. He also found that 58% of predatory journal editors in his study samples were from India.
2 Akça and Akbulut (2018) found that 55% (693) of single-journal publishers on Beall's list were in India.
3 Shamseer *et al.* (2017) found that 43% of all publishers in their study showed contact addresses in India.
4 Beall (2016a) pointed to Hyderabad, India as one of the most corrupt cities in the world where numerous predatory publishers and conference organizers are located.
5 Xia *et al.* (2015) discovered 77% of their sampled authors publishing in predatory journals were from India.
6 Shen and Björk (2015) assessed 27% of predatory publishers as being in India, and for single-journal publishers, the percentage was 42%.

Next to India, the other most common countries for predatory publishers include Pakistan, Nigeria, Iran, Malaysia, Turkey, the UAE, Indonesia, and Saudi Arabia (Erfanmanesh & Pourhossein, 2017). The distribution is heavily skewed towards South Asia, the Middle East, and North Africa, while the Americas, Europe, and the Pacific have disproportionately little representation. This is in contrast with the locations of non-predatory OA publishers. The Directory of Open Access Journals (DOAJ) whitelist has publishers spread relatively equally across continent and region.

In a cross-country study by Macháček and Srholec (2021), the total predatory articles in a country were calculated against the total of all publications of the country, revealing that Kazakhstan and Indonesia have the highest percentage of predatory publications. This study found that countries with large research sectors, but a medium level of economic development, tend to be most susceptible to predatory practices. South Asia, North Africa, and Arabic countries fall into this category.

Other studies reveal that the geographic patterns of predatory publishers may vary from discipline to discipline (Crawford, 2017; Wallace & Perri, 2018). For example, it is found that Iran, rather than India, has led predatory publishing in the field of economics, while Albania dominates social science, and China is the most active country in health sciences. Such studies, however, provide only snapshots of the findings in time rather than presenting a picture of consistent practices.

4.3.2 Warehouse publishing

It is easy to start a predatory publishing business: "you don't need any investment, you don't need any overhead, all you need is a website" (Deprez & Chen, 2017). Although this is an oversimplified statement, technology does provide the flexibility for anyone to become an online publisher if you do not care about building mature infrastructure and investing in all areas of publishing service, and most importantly, if you do not care about the scholarly quality of your products. The minimum requirement for setting up a publishing company is to purchase a domain name. Designing a website requires only basic computer skills, because many journal management applications have been created as open-source software for free download and use. Predatory publishers have frequently used a system called Open Journal Systems, which offers a comprehensive tool for the management of a journal's submission and editorial workflow, as well as the online publishing of articles and issues. With this system, predatory publishers can create an easy template and launch multiple journals at once. The so-called "template journals" are assembly-line products, characterized by a similar look of their websites and a herd of individual journals by the same publisher (Crawford, 2017).

The identical design of template journals is also widely visible across publishers. Bolshete (2018) examined the websites of 13 predatory publishers and found a high level of similarity in the layout and content of all publishers. According to him, "overall, the look and feel of all 13 publishers was similar including names of publishers, website addresses, homepage content, homepage images, list of journals and subject areas, as if they were copied and pasted" (p. 157). Other similarities include that all these journals (i) hide their contact details, (ii) provide identical author instructions, (iii) produce light content because of scant submissions, and (iv) list editorial members who serve multiple journals simultaneously, e.g., one name is listed as an editorial member 81 times for 69 journals (twice in 12 journals). Predatory publishers tend to share comparable attributes in the design of their infrastructure and the characteristics of their exploitative behaviors, but vary widely in other areas of their operations.

Some studies assume a genealogical relationship in the operations of predatory publishing: the employees of a profitable publisher may quit with experience, network, and greed to open their own business and compete with their former employer. For instance, the publisher MedCrave is viewed as "a clone of OMICS International in the sense that it copies their predatory, exploitative, and dishonest business practices" (Beall, 2016b). A commenter on scholaroa.org suggested a link between MedCrave and the OMICS International (OMICS) because one individual was found to promote both businesses on LinkedIn. When many publishing houses cluster in one small location, it is possible to observe the genealogical relationship. For example, the city of Hyderabad, India, is "home to countless predatory open-access publishers" (Beall, 2016a).

MedCrave did not officially deny the accusations, although some of the company's blog posts describe the inclusion of its name on the predatory publisher list as a rumor and fake news (e.g., Medium.com, 2018). However, MedCrave did not respond to cases introduced by individuals who introduce their own experience with MedCrave to warn authors about publishing in its journals (e.g., Kasprak, 2017; Kaye, 2017; Reichart, 2017).

4.3.3 Anatomy of selected publishers

Beall's publisher blacklist contains more than 1,000 names. Some are noticeable due to their level of severity, size of business, and other factors. For example, some large-scale publishers have gone on and off the blacklist, such as MDPI and Hindawi, creating controversies in the publishing industry; others constantly challenge Beall and his former employer, such as OMICS and Frontiers, directly resulting in the disappearance of his blacklists. Two publishers are introduced here to illustrate different paths of these practices.

a) MDPI

MDPI is a Switzerland-based publisher of OA journals. It is a good example of the heterogenous practices of scholarly publishing, being blacklisted by Beall and then taken off his publisher list. It has a combination of varied scholarly quality across journals, some of which have been indexed by the Web of Science (WoS) with a journal impact factor (JIF) value and have become recognized titles in corresponding academic fields, while others may continue accepting low quality publications. Overall, MDPI has an improved reputation, which is evidenced by a steady increase in the citation rates, favorable view of its publications, and revenue numbers year after year (Petrou, 2020).

In the early 2010s, MDPI's practices drew criticism for publishing pseudo-science articles, and came onto Beall's radar when he documented its misconduct. He called MDPI a *salon des refusés* that tended to accept fringe and junk science that other legitimate publishers would not consider. MDPI was added to Beall's blacklist in early 2014 with the following issues.

1. Using the names of reputable scholars on its editorial boards, including Nobel laureates, without their consent.
2. Creating a large fleet of journals with high APCs and a broad subject coverage.
3. Accepting as many submissions as possible.
4. Focusing on exploiting Chinese authors who have the desire to publish in "international" journals.
5. Not allowing its editors to do editorial work.
6. Publishing controversial articles to increase visibility and citation rates.
7. Misusing "institute" as the publisher's name.

Immediately, Beall's website received many comments that defended MPDI. Beall (2014a) believed these commenters to be beneficiaries or friends of the publisher, because most of the commenters were either non-scholars or scholars who had never published a paper in MDPI's journals.

MDPI decided to rehabilitate its image by retracting plagiarized and non-sense publications, and subsequently appealed to Beall with evidence of improvements (MDPI, 2014). Beall was apparently convinced and removed its name from his blacklist. MDPI has since experienced a remarkable growth in business and abundant improvements in publication quality (Petrou, 2020). Petrou's analysis revealed an increase in citations of its articles, the scholarly reputation of its journals, and the attitude of researchers toward submitting to and accepting its publications. As of early 2021, 74 of MDPI's 321 journals were provided a JIF value by WoS, indicating an acceptance by the mainstream. MDPI's leading journals are as citable as that of the average publications in their respective fields. The publisher has adopted various strategies to promote its business in both quality and quantity.

First, it has developed a speedy publishing process, with a median time from submission to publication significantly shorter than other OA publishers, an average of 39 days in 2019 (Petrou, 2020). The publisher attributes its fast performance to a fine-tuned business model that relies on its in-house team to work on tedious tasks and push and negotiate with editors, reviewers, and authors to meet deadlines. MDPI has expanded at a great rate. By 2019, it became the largest OA publisher in the world, with 110,000 papers per annum, including 103,000 research papers and reviews. In the same year, it was also ranked fifth among all publishers with respect to its journal article output. As a comparison, it was the 17th largest publisher in 2015. With its more than 2,100 employees, MDPI projected a revenue of $190–230 million USD for 2020, assuming its average discounted APCs of about $1,500 USD.

Second, it has adopted a celebrity effect model. Using its journal *Publications* as an example, Beall (2014b) described how Peter Suber, a prominent figure in OA advocacy, was cited as its editorial member. Although Suber did not stay long in that post, his name helped the journal recruit recognized scholars to its editorial board, attract high-quality submissions, invite serious reviewers, and draw more citations. The journal is now indexed by DOAJ and earned DOAJ a seal.

Moreover, MDPI has published a large number of special issues. Table 4.2 shows the number of special issues by randomly selecting MDPI journals that have a JIF value. Each of them publishes semi-monthly regular issues, but at the same time produces thousands of special issues. For example, *Sustainability* has already published 1,421 special issues and scheduled another 3,292 special issues up to 2024. The regular publications of *Sustainability* are under rigorous review to earn MPDI scholarly prestige, while its special issues allow the publisher to amass wealth. This is evidenced by the fact that only data about its regular issues are provided to WoS for the calculation of its citation rates and JIF. Future studies are needed to examine the quality of content in the special issues (Barrington *et al.*, 2020; de Vrieze, 2018).

b) OMICS International

One of the most debatable and fastest-growing OA publishers is the OMICS International, which was created in 2008 in Hyderabad, India. It cost the creator 200 rupees, less than $3 USD, to buy a domain, with which he built a website and started his publishing business. The original name of the

Table 4.2 Numbers of special issues by selected MDPI journals as of early 2021

Journal	Regular issue	Special issue		JIF
	Annual	Closed	Open	
International Journal of Molecular Sciences	24	2,115	1,855	4.556
Sustainability	24	1,421	3,292	2.576
Sensors	24	1,415	1,490	3.275
Molecules	24	1,166	1,357	3.267
Applied Sciences	24	1,032	2,204	2.474
International Journal of Environmental Research and Public Health	24	981	1,674	2.849
Energies	24	920	1,854	2.702

company was OMICS Online Publishing (Deprez & Chen, 2017). The company had its first publication, the *Journal of Proteomics & Bioinformatics*, in 2008. Two years later, it expanded into a large company that provided 68 journals, mostly in the fields of health sciences. Beall (2010) listed it on his publisher blacklist in 2010 due to its practices, such as a large proportion of empty journals (Cohen, 2015). OMICS sent Beall a letter in 2013 to seek a $1 billion USD lawsuit in damages that Beall's list created to the company (New, 2013). The letter accused Beall's judgment of being ridiculous, baseless, and impertinent. It demanded that Beall delete relevant content from his website.

In April 2013, the US Department of Health and Human Services sent a cease-and-desist letter to notify OMICS of the allegation of a trademark violation. It requested OMICS to stop using the names of the National Institutes of Health (NIH), its Institutes, PubMed Central, and any NIH employees in any erroneous and/or misleading manner (Kaiser, 2013). PubMed Central stopped indexing all journals by OMICS. In March 2017, Scopus also decided to remove multiple OMICS journals from its index over publication concerns (McCook, 2017).

Criticism of OMICS's publishing has been extensive, pointing to many areas of its practice. The following citations are a few negative reviews of this publisher about its alleged false use of scientists' names as editors.

1 OMICS allegedly listed NIH-funded scientists as editors without their knowledge, and provided incorrect information about its editors. For example, Raymond Dionne, listed by OMICS as editor-in-chief for one of its journals, is listed as scientific director of the National Institute of Nursing Research, although he is no longer working there and explicitly told OMICS not to use his NIH affiliation (Kaiser, 2013).
2 A professor of orthopedics at AIIMS-Delhi in India made a police complaint against OMICS because his name was listed as the editor of one of its journals without his consent. His allegation was echoed by several other Indian scientists whose names were also falsely listed by OMICS as editors (Yadav, 2018).
3 If anyone is placed on OMICS's editor or editorial board list but wants to resign from it, the process can be very long, if not impossible. The publisher itself admits it, citing a complicated exit process, as holding the position is considered an honor and one must "have a valid reason" to leave (Stratford, 2012).

OMICS's misconduct in many areas of its publishing has been reported. For example, the *Indian Express* found at least 177 OMICS journals without an International Standard Serial Number (ISSN) (Yadav, 2018). Also,

Table 4.3 The face value of the APC rates by OMICS's journals in US dollars

Journals	APC			
	Lowest	Highest	Mean	Median
699	$150	$3,779	$1,019	$1,139

Source: omicsonline.org, as of March 2021

many OMICS journals cover very broad scientific fields. Some OMICS journals give their publications names identical to established ones, e.g., the *Journal of Biomedical Sciences* is the same as the title of a BioMed Central publication, except that OMICS adds an "s" to make "science" plural. The *Journal of Preventive Medicine by OMICS* is similar to *Preventive Medicine*, an established journal by Elsevier. OMICS is found to often overlook peer review (Jump, 2014). For example, it published a self-plagiarized paper, with about 90% of its content identical to another paper the same author published before. This author has seven other articles being retracted by a German journal alone in 2012 for breaching the rules on "plagiarism and redundant or concurrent publication" (Jump, 2014), but has remained as an editorial member for at least five OMICS journals.

Unsurprisingly, publishing with OMICS's journals entails APCs. The fee scheme is available on the publisher's webpage for each journal (Butler, 2013). However, the rate is different from that of the website of individual journals: the latter is much higher. For example, the APCs for the *Journal of Space Exploration* is listed as $150 USD for each research or review article on the publisher's website, but on the journal's website, it is €891 (roughly $1,059 USD). Unlike most standalone journals on Beall's blacklist that charge low APCs, OMICS's journals have a high price tag across the board (Table 4.3).

The publisher has expanded into several regions of the world, including the UK, Singapore, and Canada, and has acquired multiple subsidiaries. Indian government documents show that OMICS had a revenue of $11.6 million USD and profits of $1.2 million USD in 2016. As of early 2021, OMICS published up to 700 journals, with 50,000+ editorial board members and reviewers and more than 15 million readers.

Two journalists from *Bloomberg Businessweek* visited OMICS's headquarter in India in 2017. Their report on OMICS's operations provides some insight into the daily routines of one of its employees, Prachi Tyagi, with evidence of the practices that readers may find familiar:

> Omics recruited her last year as assistant managing editor overseeing the *International Journal of Clinical Rheumatology* and the *Journal of Clinical & Experimental Pharmacology* . . . One of Tyagi's most

important tasks is soliciting manuscripts. "Sending emails is a must daily," she says. She scours Google and university websites for the addresses of academics and researchers. The signature on her correspondence with a U.S. reporter says she's based in the Los Angeles suburb of Westlake Village. For years, researchers have noted emails purporting to come from Nevada and England, where Omics has nothing more than mailboxes. Researchers on the receiving end of all those emails sent by Tyagi and an army of her fellow workers have a word for them: spam.

(Deprez & Chen, 2017)

4.4 Legal challenges

4.4.1 Against predatory publishers

In April 2019, the US Federal Trade Commission (FTC) revealed that a federal district court judge required OMICS and its owner to pay more than $50.1 million USD to resolve FTC's charges that the company made false assertions about the publishing of their conferences and journals and lied about excessive APCs (US District Court, 2019). In addition to the judgment, a federal judge in the State of Nevada, where OMICS was incorporated in 2012, asked the company to stop its predatory business practices, ordering it to provide the information of APCs and make its business transparent to authors and users.

The court ruling resolves the FTC's complaint in 2016 that alleged OMICS and its owner deceptively promoted its online journals and conferences in the fields of health science without providing authors and conference participants with rigorous peer review and editorial services as promised. During the lawsuit, the FTC successfully proved that OMICS's practices were deceptive, presenting evidence of consumer complaints, screen captures of false representation on the publisher's website, and expert testimonies about the standards of academic publishing. The court ordered OMICS to comply with future FTC demands for information, present compliance reports to the FTC for 20 years, and distribute a copy of the judgment to all its managers for five years.

The amount requested by the FTC was a calculation of what the company netted from its customers between 25 August 2011 and 31 July 2017. The *FTC v. OMICS* case was one of the first judgments in US history where the FTC sued a scholarly publisher and won the lawsuit, and is definitely the first for a predatory publisher (Manley, 2019). The verdict was by all means a victory for the academic community, and delivered a strong message to publishers who employ the same practices as OMICS, particularly those that reside in the US.

OMICS subsequently appealed the judgment. On 11 September 2020, the U.S. Court of Appeals, Ninth Circuit, upheld the FTC's $50.1 million victory. The court believed that the evidence of OMICS's deception is ample and overwhelming, and the "general denials" by OMICS and its owner are not adequate to counter that evidence. The court declared that "OMICS's misrepresentations were material and their net impression was likely to, and did in fact, deceive ordinary consumers" (Manatt, 2020). The court also stated that the owner "is personally liable for OMICS's violations because he had authority over OMICS and either had knowledge of the companies' misrepresentations or was recklessly indifferent to their truth or falsity" (Manatt, 2020). Therefore, the decision by the district judge was appropriate (Hostetler, 2020).

Manley (2020) pointed to the disagreements of both sides on professional standards in scholarly publishing. The decisions by the US District Court and the US Court of Appeals provide clear answers to these questions.

4.4.2 By predatory publishers

Publishers are aware of the impact of Beall's blacklist on businesses. When a name is added to the list, the publisher will become nervous and angry, and try to get its name removed. Appealing to Beall for removal by providing evidence that his decision was incorrect, or that improvements had been made, was one way to reach an agreement. When such an appeal was unsuccessful, the publisher may have started threatening legal action or harassing Beall verbally and in writing. OMICS's threat of a $1 billion USD lawsuit and three years in prison is an example. The publisher threatened to sue Beall for defamation under section 66A of India's Information Technology Act, 2000. This Section 66A "makes it illegal to use a computer to publish 'any information that is grossly offensive or has menacing character' or to publish false information" (New, 2013). However, OMICS did not actually proceed with the lawsuit. Two years later, Section 66A was struck down by India's Supreme Court because of an unrelated case (Sriram, 2015).

New (2013) also mentioned a lawsuit against Beall for including the Canadian Center of Science and Education and three of its related companies on his publisher blacklist. It appears that the Center also did not proceed with its lawsuit. Beall (2017) described his experience with this type of lawsuit:

> Often owners of predatory publishing operations would email me, extolling the virtues of their journals, describing the rigor of their peer review and the credentials of their esteemed editorial boards. Some of them did a self-analysis using the criteria document I used and made available, and without exception these self-analyses found that the

publisher didn't meet any of the criteria – not even close – and deserved to be removed from the list immediately.

(Beall, 2017, p. 275)

Other aggressive actions were also taken, such as contacting Beall's university and sending annoying emails attacking his products and credentials. Frontiers Media, a Switzerland-based OA publisher, is believed to have played a large role in pressuring the university to open a research-misconduct case against Beall, according to the *Chronicle* (Basken, 2017; see also Schneider, 2017). It filed a complaint that was "unique in its composition, length, detail, and complexity" (Basken, 2017), so the university undertook a formal investigation against Beall's alleged misconduct. Although the conclusion was "no findings" and no action was taken against him, Beall was under tremendous pressure, and decided to cease his anti-predatory publishing effort. He removed all his blacklists from scholarlyoa.org in January 2017 (Beall, 2017).

4.5 Government actions against predatory publishing

The proliferation of predatory publishing has reached such a level that many countries have decided to take action to address it. The negative effects have been huge, not only on research and education, but also on medical and other practices through eroding the credibility of scientific literature. For example, publications with misinformation about COVID-19 studies surged in predatory journals when the disease reached its peak in 2020 (Vervoort *et al.*, 2020). Low-quality, biased, and fraudulent studies have an adverse impact on decision-making. If the globalization efforts of every country in the realm of science aim to increase that country's visibility in a field, no one wants the visibility to be unfavorable. Some governments are pioneers in changing their policies and priorities to combat these exponentially growing activities. Unlike institutional guidelines, high-level government policies are characterized by their inflexibility and lack of granularity, and can easily become debatable when they are applied to individual situations.

4.5.1 India

As an international hub of predatory publishing, India has been facing serious challenges. Its government has vowed to strike back against predatory behaviors in scholarly research. Promising the parliament that "we will end this menace of predatory journals" (Priyadarshini, 2018), the minister in charge of higher education urged universities to revise their guidelines for scholarly journals to be included in the whitelist developed by the University Grants Commission (UGC).

The UGC maintains a whitelist of reputable journals for institutions, individuals, publishers, and associations to follow. The original list, including many dubious journals, was revised to remove over 3,000 journals and became the UGC-CARE Reference List of Quality Journals in 2018 (Patwardhan, 2019). The UGC also facilitates inter-institutional and transdisciplinary collaborations by teaming up with the government and academic leaders to form a consortium and promote more awareness about scientific integrity and publishing ethics among students and researchers. It invites its consortium members, over 30 statutory councils, to "identify, continuously monitor, and maintain a reference list of quality journals across disciplines" (Tao, 2020), and organizes workshops and conferences to discuss and advocate the importance of scientific conduct. A course on academic integrity was designed as a requirement of the pre-PhD curriculum, and aimed to educate young generations of scholars about the consequences of publishing with predatory journals. The efforts have resulted in some positive changes, e.g., observed improvement of journals in their operations.

However, there are still challenges, such as the problem of capturing citations in Indian languages and the difficulty in controlling the quality of journals in the humanities and arts. The largest challenge still comes from individual authors who are inclined to seek easy resume items to bolster their careers, an attitude cultivated within the academic publishing culture in India. Until the government implements more stringent rules to regulate publishing and institutions cooperate with the authorities to fortify the assessment of scientific research, there is still a long way to go.

4.5.2 South Africa

South African authors are found to publish five times more predatory articles than authors in the US, and two-and-a-half times more than Chinese researchers (Macháček & Srholec, 2021). Since 2011, predatory publishing in South Africa has jumped more than 140-fold in six years (Mouton & Valentine, 2017). The South African government decided to take actions to regulate academic conduct. One change was to withhold a great amount of money in subsidies and redistribute funds for institutions, so "if an institution was affected by a predatory journal publication, it would not receive the units and the money for those units would be redistributed to the entire budget" (Naidu & Dell, 2019).

Another change was to establish a trusted list of publishers and journals. The Department of Higher Education and Training (DHET) announced its recognition of six journal indexes, including WoS, the International Bibliography of the Social Sciences, Scopus, the Norwegian Register for Scientific Journals (Level 2), SciELO SA, and the DHET list. The last two are

South Africa-based. Each year, DHET distributes a new list based upon an analysis of the six indexes for subsidy allocations. DHET collaborates with other government agencies, including the National Research Foundation, Academy of Science of South Africa, and Council on Higher Education, to organize workshops to address and educate people on scholarly publishing (Hedding, 2019).

Further, various government agencies work together with higher education institutions to investigate individual cases of predatory publishing and penalize those who are found to have engaged in scientific misconduct. As a result of active interventions by the government, the extent of predatory publishing has been reduced recently, particularly in subsidy-earning journals. For example, there were 180 identified predatory publications by South African authors in 2016, but only 125 were submitted for 2017 subsidies (Naidu & Dell, 2019).

4.5.3 China

With a tiny number of predatory publishers and journals, China benefits from the language barriers and the government's early efforts in cracking down on problem publications (Lin & Zhan, 2014). However, China has a large number of predatory authors. The government is aware of the issue and has taken various steps to improve research integrity and reduce low-quality or deceitful publications. The government has discussed national policies for discouraging researchers from, or penalizing them for, submitting articles to predatory journals (Cyranoski, 2018a). The government announced a proposal for developing a journal blacklist in 2018, although neither the criteria nor the actual list have been completed since then, for various reasons.

The government revised its policies later that same year. It set an extensive punishment mechanism that will be implemented by the joint force of several government agencies (Cyranoski, 2018b). One of the changes is the development of a "social credit system," with which one's misconduct could result in restrictions or penalties on his/her other activities, such as the suspension of research projects, termination of research funds, or delay of promotion. The effectiveness of these policies will depend on how the government defines misconduct and enforces the policies.

4.5.4 Brazil and Indonesia

Brazil has a smaller share of predatory publications compared to the BRICS countries, and also compared to some other countries with active predatory publishing ecosystems, such as Nigeria, Iran, and several Middle East countries. This is largely because of the journal ranking system, Qualis, that the Brazil government has invested in (Jeffé, 2020), which ranks graduate programs from different subject areas and promotes selected national journals. As a system that focuses on journals from within Brazil, managed by chosen experts, and encouraged for use by the authority, Qualis has served to guide authors in selecting publishing outlets in recognized local journals and limiting the opportunities for predatory publications.

Qualis has its limitations, though. It has lowered the standard of Brazilian science, because publishing in journals of varying quality within the system provides academics the same amount of credit. Authors are incentivized to publish in lower-tier journals for easy acceptance of submissions. Once predatory journals manage to slip into the system, which seems inevitable, they immediately become popular. Perlin *et al.* (2018) observed a sudden increase in the number of predatory articles by Brazilian authors in response to the inclusion of predatory journals in Qualis. Researchers advocate for the Brazilian government to (i) take an international scope by adopting globally established standards, (ii) refine the structure of the Qualis system, and (iii) strengthen the journal evaluation and inclusion process.

Indonesia is a world leader regarding the number of OA journals (Reynold, 2020). It also makes the most contributions, alongside Kazakhstan, to predatory publications (Macháček & Srholec, 2021). Because of this development, the Indonesian government passed a law in 2019, the National Knowledge System and Technology, promoting public access to research results and encouraging transparency in scholarship dissemination. With regard to predatory publishing, the government recently changed its policies for assessing promotions, in order to pressure academics to publish in reliable outlets. Positive results will not be available until the government has completely implemented the new policies (Sabarini, 2021).

4.6 Conclusion

The discussion of predatory publishers is intertwined with that of predatory journals, as both are evaluated and categorized with a similar set of criteria and can hardly be separated. They share the same characteristics within the ecosystem of scholarly publishing. However, each has its own characteristics. This chapter has attempted to explore the concept, history, and current conditions of predatory publishers, providing an understanding of their development from a geopolitical perspective, a socioeconomic position, and a legal viewpoint. It described the dynamics of scholarly conduct and diverse individual reactions to the changing environment.

The description of government efforts in several countries echoes the arguments in the previous descriptions of reasons for the prosperity of predatory businesses. This chapter aimed to express that although these countries have historically set unsuitable policies to pressure authors into scholarly publishing, which resulted in scientific misconduct, they have also recently changed their approaches by revising relevant policies to emphasize quality over quantity.

5 Stakeholders

Journal publishing is a joint effort between publishers, who build viable infrastructure, and other stakeholders, including editors and editorial boards who manage evaluations, authors who contribute content, reviewers who safeguard the quality of manuscripts, and readers who use and cite publications. Rigorous work by all constituencies is required to produce a reputable journal to promote scholarship. In predatory publishing, unfortunately, every party has engaged in distorted work and therefore has contributed to the proliferation of scientifically disputed material in predatory journals. The previous chapters have discussed publishers' practices, leaving this chapter to examine the participation of other players in the predatory publishing business.

5.1 Authors

If, according to Shen and Björk (2015), predatory journals worldwide had published as many as 420,000 articles by 2014, a significant number of authors must have engaged in predatory publishing. With an ever-increasing number of predatory journals since then, one would expect many more articles have been published afterwards, by a commensurately increasing number of authors. People may be curious about who these authors are, their geographic distribution, why they choose to publish in predatory journals, and whether they are aware of the characteristics of predatory publishing.

5.1.1 Who are predatory authors?

The early literature was inclined to describe the prototypical author who published in a predatory journal as someone from a developing country where economic conditions are disadvantaged, infrastructure of scholarly communication is poor, and the dominant academic language is not English (e.g., Nwagwu, 2016; Truth, 2012). The emerging globalization advocacy in many third-world

DOI: 10.4324/9781003029335-5

countries in the 1980s sparked a series of reforms in governmental and institutional policies that pressed researchers to publish in English-language international journals, thereby providing the countries with fertile soil for predatory publishing. It is thus reasonable to expect more predatory authors there.

Predatory journals are notorious for their low standards of manuscript acceptance. Their tolerance of broken language and grammar makes them well suited to exophonic writers, and their lax, if any, peer review has galvanized those who do not have the necessary training or experience to complete publishable articles. When publish-or-perish pressure becomes more critical for those who need to survive tenure evaluations than for their senior colleagues, more young and inexperienced researchers take advantage of the possibilities of predatory publishing (Shaw, 2013). Junior scholars have also been described as less knowledgeable about how to distinguish a predatory journal from a legitimate publication.

This portrait of the typical author has been supported by evidence (e.g., Frandsen, 2017; Truth, 2012). Truth described a geographic distribution of predatory authors in lower-income economies in Africa, South Asia, and the Middle East. Another study (Xia et al., 2015) explored author profiles of selected predatory journals. A total of 941 authors were analyzed for their publications and citations, academic rankings, and geographic locations, which were then compared to authors who published in various groups of non-predatory open access (OA) journals, i.e., one group of journals showing rigorous peer review in Bohannon's sting operation and registered with the Directory of Open Access Journals (DOAJ), and another group from the Public Library of Science (PLOS) series that had been recognized as high-quality publications. All groups were OA journals, required article processing charges (APCs), and fell in the field of biomedicine. Furthermore, corresponding authors were studied to understand how the selections of publishing outlets are made, because corresponding authors often make intellectual contributions to a study and decide where to submit manuscripts (Perlin et al., 2018).

Unlike authors in the other two groups, most authors in predatory journals had no publication history. Their citation counts were also significantly different than the comparison groups, who had accrued many more citations. Even for corresponding authors, those in predatory journals had very few publications and citations. The authors who published in predatory journals were considered essentially young scholars, such as doctoral students and junior researchers, with limited research experience and training. Based on their work affiliation, these authors were primarily from South Asia, the Middle East, and Africa. Three countries were particularly noticeable: India (77%), Nigeria (9%), and Pakistan (5%). On the other hand, authors in the non-predatory group were largely from East Asian countries, such as South

Korea, and Italy; authors in the PLOS series were mainly from industrialized countries, including the US, the UK, and Australia.

India has contributed the most predatory authors (Shen & Björk, 2015; Xia et al., 2015). Seethapathy et al. (2016) examined over 3,000 articles in 350 predatory journals authored by Indians to see which categories of educational and research institutions their corresponding authors fall into. Using UGC's guidelines that codes universities into central, state, private, private colleges, and government colleges and by research type, the study found that more than half of predatory authors from India were from government and private colleges. The rest included private (18%), state (15%), national (11%), and central (3%) colleges. The numbers indicate that lower-level and instruction-oriented institutions are the most active in predatory publishing.

Indonesia is another active country. Kozok (2017, 2020) studied journals by an Azerbaijan-based business that shows predatory practices, with a lax review process, and asks for relatively low APCs. Indonesian authors account for 20% of the authors. They are exclusively from smaller and less prestigious institutions of higher education. For example, authors from the State University of Makassar are particularly visible, comprising 13% of the authors. Some of the journals even hire Indonesian scholars as their co-editors.

An analysis of 34 OA journals produced by two publishers in Nigeria was conducted by Nwagwu (2016). These publishers are all included in Beall's list of predatory publishers in 2012. This study of 5,599 authors revealed an overwhelming percentage of the authors (87.3%) were from 75 non-industrial countries. Table 5.1 lists the top ten countries that contribute the most predatory authors:

Table 5.1 Top ten countries with predatory authors

Country	Number	Percent
Nigeria	889	21.60%
China	849	20.63%
India	634	15.41%
Iran	522	12.68%
Pakistan	382	9.28%
Malaysia	215	5.22%
Turkey	189	4.59%
Saudi Arabia	153	3.72%
Brazil	146	3.55%
South Africa	136	3.30%

(Source: Modified from Nwagwu, 2016, Table 2)

With a rapid expansion of predatory publications, however, the authorship has diversified. Over time, seasoned scholars have become increasingly active. There has been a growth of authors beyond low-prestige, instruction-oriented universities, for example:

1. Most Iranian authors publishing in predatory journals are from a small handful of top-ranked universities. Nearly 71% have an affiliation with Islamic Azad University, which is ranked second in Iran. The top-ranked University of Tehran contributes more than 5% of the predatory authorship. These authors' institutions are all "among the most reputable and well-known universities of the country" (Erfanmanesh & Pourhossein, 2017, p. 440).
2. In China, even though the names of recognized scholars have not commonly appeared in the first author and corresponding author list, there has been an obvious increase in the number of senior researchers who make observable contributions to predatory publications (Xu et al., 2020).
3. Wallace and Perri (2018) studied the publishing pattern of selected economists and found that almost 22% of the registered authors in the renowned repository RePEc have contributed to predatory journals. Many are seasoned scholars whose median publication history is six years. A startling number of the top 5% of RePEc authors have participated in predatory publishing, and their predatory articles consist of 4.9% of their total publications. Table 5.2 shows the geographic distributions of these economists.

Furthermore, predatory authors are no longer the exclusively from developing countries. More scholars from wealthy countries have joined the group. For example, a study examining authorship in more than 200 predatory journals in biomedical science found that more than half of the articles had corresponding authors from "high- and upper-middle-income

Table 5.2 Top five countries of predatory authors in economics

Country	Number	Percent
Iran	279	10.06%
US	218	7.88%
Nigeria	204	7.34%
Malaysia	186	6.69%
Turkey	176	6.34%

Source: Wallace & Perri, 2018

countries as defined by the World Bank" (Moher *et al.*, 2017, p. 23). Predatory authors from the US made the second most contributions (15%), second only to India (27%). Similarly, Wallace and Perri (2018) found that the US contributes the second-largest group of economists in predatory journals (Table 5.2).

A study of German authors who published in pseudo-scientific journals identified as many as 5,000 scientists, including some prominent professors, such as a university president and top scientists in major pharmaceutical companies (NDR, 2018). Although the authors claimed that they were unaware of the predatory nature of the journals, the public was still astonished by the rate of penetration in Germany. The predatory authors were publicly criticized, and the story was widely broadcast on the radio, podcast via the Internet, and published in newspapers. By doing so, critics hoped to prevent such low-quality work from happening in the future.

Similar studies found predatory authorship in many other Western countries. For example, about 5% of Italian researchers were found to publish in journals listed by Beall's blacklist (Bagues *et al.*, 2019), and faculty in a Canadian business school have extensively used their articles in predatory outlets for promotion (Pyne, 2017).

To be fair, even if a more diverse authorship has been observed, most predatory authors are still young, less-privileged scholars in developing countries. For example, even though many top economists have published in predatory journals, their articles comprise only a small percentage of their total publications (Wallace & Perri, 2018). Studies on author profiles have extensively named developing countries as the major sources of predatory authorship. Countries like India, Nigeria, Pakistan, Iran, Malaysia, and China are always on the top of such lists. Despite the visibility of some developed countries, particularly the US, the proportion of their predatory authors to the total academic workforce is negligible.

5.1.2 Why do authors publish in predatory journals?

There has been a continuous debate about whether authors know a journal is predatory when they submit their work to it. The literature reveals that researchers are generally unaware of the unprofessional misconduct of some new OA journals and, thus, are innocent victims of predatory publishing (e.g., Truth, 2012). Once they submit their papers to, or agree to serve on the editorial board of, any journal that is involved in deceptive practices, it will be too late for them to undo their actions. Many do not realize the unethical practices of predatory journals they submit papers to until they are billed for acceptance and publication of their papers, while such payment information was typically not previously available.

A small-scale survey of authors who published in predatory journals in criminal justice science showed that one-third of the respondents were aware of the term "predatory journal," but only one respondent connects the term to Beall's predatory journal list (Noga-Styron et al., 2017). The respondents had mixed feelings about asking their articles to be withdrawn or about publishing in such journals again, indicating their poor knowledge of the negative consequences for scientific credibility and personal reputation. Also, when asked if their publications in predatory journals were used for tenure and promotion reviews, the answers were all positive, indicating they unwittingly published there. A similar finding was made by another survey of authors in Bangladesh (Shuva & Taisir, 2016).

Not only have surveys exposed the naivete of many authors about predatory publishing, but the media has also introduced cases where individual academics give testimonies about their unfortunate experiences. For example, a doctoral student at Louisiana State University sent her research to a journal that invited her to submit articles, and received an $1,800 invoice in return (Stratford, 2012). *Science Magazine* published a similar story wherein an assistant professor described how he responded to an invitation and ended up publishing in a predatory journal (Chambers, 2019). He was aware of predatory publishing, but did not find the title of the inviting journal in Beall's blacklist. He regretted not paying attention to many typical predatory behaviors by the journal.

Those who have fallen prey to predatory publishing may experience emotional turmoil after recognizing their situations. The emotions may include shock, dismay, disappointment, and anger (Rawas et al., 2020). Many have tried to recover by asking to withdraw their manuscripts, but very few such requests are granted. When Chambers (2019) asked to withdraw immediately after his submission, he was urged to pay a withdrawal fee as well as an APC, because his paper was published regardless.

Other evidence, however, seems to draw a more complex picture of predatory authorship, where people who publish in such journals are described as knowing participants (Ray, 2016). Predatory publishing has been in practice for more than a decade, and its existence and visible tricks have already become known to academics and the public; regardless, predatory journals keep growing in the market. Such a constant growth is impossible without scholars being complicit in making active contributions. Authors' deliberate involvement has been increasingly described in literature (Beall, 2017; Frandsen, 2019). Critics even raise doubts about the claims of ignorance by predatory authors.

In their 2012 survey of a group of professors from two Nigerian national universities, Omobowale et al. (2014) found out why they decided to publish in predatory journals. All interviewees pointed to the standard specified by the local university appointment and promotion bodies that require academics to publish in foreign journals. Predatory journals fall in that category, and are easy to publish in for Nigerian scholars, who mostly do not have the necessary qualifications to compete with scholars in the West. Yet, no matter what reasons these interviewees express, they are all conscious of the low-quality, lax review, speedy and pay-to-publish nature of the foreign journals.

Knowing participants in predatory publishing are not limited to those in developing countries, but are also found in developed countries. A study of a Canadian school revealed the incentives for faculty to publish in shady journals (Pyne, 2017). Based on publicly available data on faculty salaries and publications, this study provided evidence of the relationships between publication quantity and the benefits of hiring, tenure, promotion, research awards, and compensation. Scholars who published in predatory journals received greater financial compensation than those publishing in non-predatory journals. Predatory publications were also found to be correlated with internal research awards. It is, thus, not surprising to observe that "the majority of faculty with research responsibilities at a small Canadian business school have publications in predatory journals" (Pyne, 2017, p. 137), including not only junior faculty but also many senior faculty members.

Similarly, the reason motivating Italian authors to take the risk of predatory publishing was their expectation of obtaining positive evaluations when being assessed by randomly selected committee members. The experience and expertise of the members determined the quality of the evaluations. The authors knew of the deceitful nature of predatory publications, but hoped that they might benefit from presenting a large quantity of publications, including easy ones. This study "suggests that the proliferation of 'predatory' journals reflects the existence of severe information asymmetries in scientific evaluations" (Bagues *et al.*, 2019, p. 462).

A survey was taken with specially designed questions to understand predatory authorship (Kurt, 2018). A grounded theory was applied to analyze the collection, transcription, and coding of answers from 96 responses. Four themes were categorized, including social identity threat, unawareness, high pressure, and lack of research proficiency. Social identity threat refers to the anxiety that one may be considered inferior to others within the same group. People from less-developed countries are more likely to have social identity threat. Threat may also be represented by religious, language, and geographic differences. Unawareness is an obvious reason in many cases, but many people continued publishing in the same journals. Pressure to publish drives people to continue their publishing efforts, especially when locals do not have the expertise and resources to separate a predatory journal from a legitimate one. Lack of research proficiency puts scholars, particularly those from less-developed countries, at a disadvantage in seeking publishing opportunities in high-quality journals. Their reliance on low-standards predatory journals is viewed as the consequence of their institutions' deficits in providing necessary academic support (Al-Khatib, 2016).

Kurt's findings provide only one theory to elucidate predatory authorship. There are many other ways to rationalize the causes. Predatory authors are categorized into those too naïve, those careless, and those pseudo-scientific (Eaton, 2018). They are also defined as those who mimic the work of others, those who need rapid publications, those who are ignorant, and those who take inadequate evaluations (Omobowale et al., 2014).

An economic model was applied to examine the supply-demand relationship of scholarly publishing (Xia, 2019). In economic theory, a market functions by equating demand and supply through a price mechanism. This study uses publication quality to replace price as the equilibrium to stabilize the number of publications versus the number of researchers at the global scale. In past decades, the growth of the researcher population created a large demand for publishing venues, particularly in many developing countries. The demand inspired a rapid development of publishing outlets, which is represented by the number of journals. The latter development tended to be so massive that it made the supply largely outnumber the demand, resulting in the spread of low-quality and exploitative publishing businesses. However, the market will follow its own rules to adjust the quality equilibrium toward a new balance. The enthusiasm for predatory publishing will cool down after some time, but it may never go away and will adjust to the level of demand.

5.2 Editors and editorial board members

In traditional scholarly publishing, editors play a critical role in guiding authors, leading the editorial board, soliciting peer reviews, connecting to the scholarly community, cooperating with journal publishers, and being responsible to the public (Council of Science Editors, 2020). In predatory publishing, peer review is negligent or nonexistent. An editor's responsibility is nowhere near what legitimate journals have asked their editors to perform in safeguarding quality. Predatory publishers are more interested in making a profit than advancing science, and so ask their editors to primarily solicit article submissions and sometimes handle minor logistic tasks. Even when editors do seek peer review, their opinions may be ignored by the publishers, whose intent is nothing more than attempting to trick authors into believing they engage in appropriate professional conduct in order to entice submissions.

Who are predatory editors? Opening the websites of predatory journals, one will find patterns in their editorial service. In some cases, particularly with standalone journals, only one managing editor is listed – presumably, the publisher who owns the business but does not have the necessary scholarly background. This was a relatively common practice in the early days of predatory publishing. Given the fact that single-journal publishers dominated the predatory market before the mid-2010s (Shen & Björk, 2015), one would expect to observe many non-academic editors at that time.

Over time, the market has experienced constant reshuffling of ownership of predatory publishers due to the unstable and competitive business model. Small publishers have gradually given way to large-sized ones that publish multiple journals. With mega-publishing, it is not unusual to observe the same editor-in-chief assigned to multiple titles under the same publisher. Such a super-editor needs to oversee publications with a broad subject coverage. This model of multi-disciplinary scope has been widely used as a key criterion to identify predatory practices that indicate poor editorial quality.

It is common that the names of predatory editors are not publicly listed at the affiliations provided. Among others, reasons for concealed identities may include predatory journals' use of fake names, fabrication of academic connections, or failure to update editorial profiles. Time and again, making up editors' names and resumes has become one of the tricks predatory publishers use to game scientific metrics.

Most commonly, however, scholars affiliated with accredited instructional and research institutions are listed as the editors and editorial members. Predatory journals adopt several strategies to recruit their editors and editorial board members. As described previously, they constantly send out spam emails to invite scholars to serve as editors, guest editors, honorary editors, or board members. Although it remains unknown how many of those invited are aware of the real practices of these inviting journals, many have indeed become editors or board members through this method of recruitment.

Predatory journals are more interested in hiring established scholars for their journals. In scholarly publishing, authors often decide the outlets for their publications based on the reputation of a journal's editorial board. However, senior scholars seem to be more hesitant about, and less interested in, doubtful experiments than their junior colleagues. Predatory journals thus use an alternate strategy: stealing the identities of senior scholars without their permission. The media and scholarly studies have widely reported cases where recognized scholars found their names on suspicious journals without any acknowledgement; for example:

1 Kozok (2017) contacted seven editors and editorial board members of a dubious journal. Of five responses, four insisted they did not have an affiliation with the journal and would ask for their names to be removed. The fifth respondent is listed as a co-editor who stated that he had never reviewed any papers, before or after these papers were published, and planned to quit his title. He seemed to know that he was listed as an editor of the journal, however.
2 A University of Washington chemist and material scientist and a Baylor University high-energy physicist expressed their shock after discovering their names among a list of 87 editorial board members on a counterfeit journal's website (Butler, 2013).

It is unknown how many scholars have served predatory journals as editors or editorial board members in total. Likewise, there is no data to reveal how many scholars whose names are affiliated with predatory journals have been aware of their identity being stolen. But in a recent study, Downes (2020) has been able to calculate the ratio of predatory editors who know the unethical nature of their journals to editors who are unaware of the practice: 1.9:1. Although Downes' focus is primarily on Australian researchers, his finding has provided a snapshot of predatory editorship.

Downes found that as many as 3,754 scholars, roughly 7% of the entire Australian academic community, have served as predatory journal editors or board members. Conducted from December 2017 to December 2019, the study examined a group of 966 alleged predatory journals for editors and editorial members. A survey was then sent to 2,342 of those whose contact information was available online. Of the 609 respondents, roughly one-third claimed that they did not engage in any editorial services, and had no idea about their names appearing on the journals, while "about two-thirds of those involved were either ignorant (or in denial) of the unethical status of their publishing hosts or were knowingly complicit" (Downes, 2020, p. 289). Downes' study becomes more informative when his examination was shifted briefly from Australian scholars to editors in six other English-speaking countries. By narrowing down the journals published by one publisher, the Science Publishing Group, he presented the following data (Table 5.3).

Another study examining 1,015 editors for journals on Beall's blacklist found that predatory journals have enlisted various types of profiles for their editorial boards (Ruiter-Lopez et al., 2019). While some editors and editorial board members were detected as fake or unqualified scholars, the

Table 5.3 Country proportions of editors serving journals by the Science Publishing Group

Country	Editors per million population
Australia	4.1
Canada	3
Ireland	2.7
Israel	5.1
New Zealand	4.8
UK	3.9
US	4.8

(Source: Modified from Downes, 2020, Table 2)

majority include highly recognized scholars from 74 different countries, nearly half of whom are in the US. The median number of publications for these editors was 43, and the median number of citations was 664, alongside a median h-index of 14. Most of the editors did not know that their names were used, and some did not even know what a predatory journal was. Not surprisingly, their names and affiliations were all visible on the websites of the journals, but their email addresses were intentionally hidden because the predatory publishers did not want authors and readers communicating directly with the unknowing editors. This study found that these journals had a median of 21 editorial members, and 78 scholars served as editors for more than one journal. One of them served as an editor for 15 journals.

To understand how predatory journals recruit their editors and editorial board members, sting operations have been conducted that used fabricated identities to apply for editors' positions (e.g., Marcus & Oransky, 2016). It was found that getting such positions is easy and fast. A systematic sting operation designed by a group of Polish scholars (Sorokowski et al., 2017) provides better insight into the predatory practice. These scholars created a profile for a fake scientist, Anna O. Szust, and sent applications to 360 journals for an editorial position. Everything in her profile was fictional, from her degrees to her publications. Szust had accounts with Academia.edu, Google+, and Twitter, and had a faculty webpage with a link on her resume. Her profile was constructed so that simple verification of any of her records would be able to detect fraudulence, and her deceitful credentials did not show necessary experience for an editorial job. Of the 360 journals to which the fictional scholar applied as an editor, one-third were indexed by WoS, one-third were from the DOAJ, and the rest were from Beall's blacklist.

Upon applying, four predatory journals immediately designated Anna O. Szust as editor-in-chief. Later, another 40 predatory journals and eight

DOAJ journals accepted her as an editor without sending her any questions or conducting any interviews. Over a dozen journals required her, or strongly encouraged her, to pay a subscription fee or make a donation, as a condition of acceptance. In addition, she was asked to publish for a fee in journals where she would become an editor. These publishers hoped to take advantage of her before considering her application. Some other journals seemed to be less aggressive and treated her more like a business partner, promising her 30% of the revenue for starting a new journal and 20% for joining an existing journal as editor, or by splitting profits with her if she could help attract papers or organize conferences, after which the conference papers would be published in proceedings with APCs required. Unsurprisingly, none of the journals that appointed her as an editor discussed with her how to review the quality of manuscripts.

As a conclusion of the sting operation, the authors emailed those journals that accepted Szust as an editor or board member. Several journals responded by denying their acceptance, claiming that they had reformed their vetting process, or blaming the unethical conduct of the study. One journal threatened to file a lawsuit. But despite the withdrawal requests, 11 journals still list Szust's name on their websites as editor, editorial board member, management staff, a conference organizing committee member, or a member of the Advisory Board of the Journals Open Access Indexing Agency.

5.3 Reviewers

Hundreds of scholars have helped review submissions for predatory journals, inadvertently or knowingly, which is informed by self-reports from academics who enter their peer-review and editing contributions for academic journals into, and verified by, Publons. As a commercial website, Publons provides a free service to track the activities of individual scientists in scholarly publishing efforts. The records in the Publons database of peer review report are credible because the website entails a verification process for all its entries. Reviewers are required to confirm their claims by forwarding e-mails of acknowledgment to Publons, or by having journal editors independently authorize their work. There are millions of records available in the Publons database, including reviews for predatory journals. A large-scale study of Publons entries (Severin *et al.*, 2020) found a total of 6,077 reviews by 738 reviewers for over 1,160 journals listed by Cabells. In other words, as many as 10% of predatory journals on Cabells's list have a review history on Publons.

There are no statistics to expose how many reviewers are aware that they are reviewing for predatory journals. Direct and indirect evidence suggests the existence of several clusters of reviewers whose motives are different. The first cluster includes scholars who may know what they are doing, but hope to shepherd research by providing guidance to unexperienced authors. Van Noorden (2020) interviewed scholars of this type, including one researcher in the UK, who helped four Nigeria-based predatory journals review eight submissions in order to improve their publication quality, and another reviewer from Germany who provided one review for a predatory journal. Not surprisingly, none of their review recommendations were accepted by the requesting publishers, according to their own descriptions, which supports the argument that predatory journals tend to accept all submitted manuscripts to maximize their profit margin, and review invitations are basically an avenue for self-promotion. Rejecting submissions is rarely an option.

The interviewees indicated that they would no longer accept invitations from predatory journals in the future. "Clearly I was naively deluded in thinking if you had proper reviews the quality of publications would rise," one of them said, regretting his service (Van Noorden, 2020). This cluster of reviewers may consist of a small number of individuals who are seasoned researchers and mainly reside in industrialized countries.

Another cluster of reviewers may also be aware that they are reviewing for shady, or at least low-quality, journals. They are young, junior researchers who have not yet established necessary academic credentials and therefore are not invited by recognized journals for reviews. Such records of contribution to science will help them build credentials that are acceptable by local standards. It is not a coincidence that these reviewers are primarily affiliated with institutions in countries in Sub-Saharan Africa, the Middle East and North Africa, and South Asia. The Publons study, however, found that a small number of these reviewers left a large number of review records per person (Severin *et al.*, 2020, Table 1). Most notably, their review activities are almost exclusively for predatory journals: one group is 76–99%, and the other is 100%.

Presumably, the majority of predatory journal reviewers are those who may not know the exact nature of their reviewed journals. Researchers tend to pay less attention to the reputation of a journal that they are reviewing for than a journal that they want to publish in. They can decide where to submit, but do not have a control over who will invite them for a review. Taking into consideration the huge number of predatory journals (e.g., more than 10,000 such titles in the Cabells's blacklist), academics seldom identify predatory titles when a review invitation is received. The reviewers of this group in the Publons study include those who contribute very few reviews for predatory journals and make far more contributions to legitimate journals (Severin *et al.*, 2020). The shares of their reviews for predatory journals are only 1–25% of the total record of their reviews available in Publons. As many as 75% of the reviewers in the records for predatory journals belong to this group. Comparatively, they are the most experienced scholars, based on their academic age and publication number.

The Publons study suggests that examining the content of reviews for predatory journals will help measure the review quality, in comparison to those for legitimate journals. However, evaluating the quality of reviews is time-consuming and subjective if the original manuscripts are not read as well. In addition, the actual content of predatory reviews is rarely discoverable, even on Publons.

It sounds like a waste of valuable time and effort for the reviewers. But if these reviewers do receive academic credit for their contribution, and if this credit is accepted by their institutions for tenure, promotion, and other career benefits, a win-win situation seems to have been created for both predatory publishers and individual reviewers. Nonetheless, the relationship is unlikely to advance science by blocking flawed or fake research; thus, the losers of this publishing practice include readers, the scholarly community, and the public.

5.4 Readers

Readership of OA publications can be identified by a combination of factors, such as citations, article-level metrics including data of views and downloads, discussions in online comments, social media, bookmarking, and recommendations (Fenner, 2013). Predatory publishers never release article-level metrics, so data about article usage is unavailable. Also, information about online or social media discussions and recommendations of predatory articles cannot be obtained. Both publishers and authors tend to keep their publications low-key. Hence, citation counts become the only measure of readership of predatory journals, as well as the scientific impact of predatory publications.

An early study of citations of predatory articles examined 32 journals published by two Nigerian publishers (Nwagwu, 2016). The analysis was based upon publications in 2012 with citations available in 2014. It was found that a total of 5,601 citable articles have received as many as 12,596 citations, roughly 2.25 citations per article. The citing sources include many countries, but mostly countries in Asia, Africa, and Europe. The top five countries with the greatest numbers of citations are India, China, Pakistan, Iran, and Malaysia.

The Nigerian case is a bit complicated because two of the journals, the *African Journal of Pharmacy and Pharmacology* and the *Journal of Medicinal Plants Research*, were once indexed by the Web of Science (WoS).

Although WoS deleted them in 2011 and 2010, respectively, the fact that they were formerly in the world-renowned database makes the interpretation of predatory readership confusing. Since academics universally trust WoS, when they read and cited articles in a WoS journal published in 2012, how many of them were aware of the removal of the journals from the database a year prior? No response was provided by the publishers.

A similar situation was found by Björk *et al.* (2020) when they identified a group of journals on Cabells's list and counted citations of their articles by searching Google Scholar. They found a few articles with sizable citation counts. By re-examining their samples, they recognized that these highly cited publications, although listed by Cabells, are actually indexed by WoS and deposited in the leading medical PubMed Central (PMC) repository. These journals were then removed from the study to make sure the results could truly explain predatory readership.

Björk *et al.* detected a high of 67% of predatory articles that have not received any citations at all. For those receiving citations, the average is 2.1 per article, which is in contrast to the average of citations to non-predatory publications. This study included comparison groups: one group with all Scopus-indexed articles, the second with Scopus-indexed articles published in OA journals, and the third with articles in born-OA journals indexed in Scopus. The three comparison groups have the average citations of 18.1, 16.5, and 12.4, respectively.

In another study, about one-third of predatory articles in an Italian sample had never been cited (Bagues *et al.*, 2019). Once again, a few articles were found to have attracted many citations, i.e., several articles each had at least 20 citations, with one article receiving 399 citations. This outlier distorts the calculation and yields a "median" of three citations per article. Unfortunately, the authors did not take any further steps to check the cause of the distortion, as Björk *et al.* did.

Anderson (2019) searched WoS, the ScienceDirect database, and PLOS One to find their citations of articles in predatory journals, as identified through various sting operations and proven to be questionable in operation and publication quality. The study shows that two of the journals do not receive any citations at all, while the other five journals receive very few, indicating that legitimate publications have rarely paid any attention to predatory articles. Of the predatory journals that did receive citations, 36% of one journal's articles had citations, the second had 25% cited articles, and the third had 6%. Altogether, it was calculated that these predatory articles had received an average rate of about 0.15 citations within 2–3 years of their publication.

All these studies provide similar findings that predatory publications have unanimously received very few citations, although the number of citations per article and the percentage of articles with citations per journal vary from study to study. Compared to the average number of citations of articles in legitimate journals, articles in predatory journals have rarely been used by readers and created negligible, if any, impact on scientific inquiry. Frandsen (2017) found that those who cite predatory articles resemble the demographics of predatory publishing authors. The citers are primarily inexperienced authors from Africa, Southeast Asia, or South Asia, and the citation rate is low. Still, she warns of the potential consequences of reading and citing predatory articles, because some experienced authors from the rest of the world are also found among the citing authors, although to a lesser extent. In many subject areas, particularly in health sciences, any spreading of pseudoscience or false discoveries may have serious consequences for human lives.

5.5 Conclusion

It takes a village to build the predatory publishing market. Predatory publishers would not be able to survive and grow without the active participation of authors, either as innocent victims or voluntary contributors. This chapter strived to piece together separate studies to understand different author groups and their reasons for publishing in predatory journals. Also, predatory editorship and reviewership are as heterogeneous as authorship, in terms of how editors are appointed and how reviewers are invited, as well as why they decide to take the responsibility and whether they are aware that they are serving low-quality or bogus publications.

Information about review and use of predatory publications is relatively difficult to obtain. However, researchers have developed smart strategies to collect direct and indirect data to help reveal these types of predatory business. Together, we can better understand the real work of the publishing enterprise from the perspective of all stakeholders, which is critical for informing scholars taking on roles as readers, authors, and possible reviewers or editors when dealing with predatory publishing.

6 Hijacked publishing

This chapter provides a snapshot of hijacked publishing by introducing its common practices. Hijacked publishing is broadly referred to as a crime, rather than unprofessional and unethical conduct, as predatory publishers and journals are often labeled (Bohannon, 2015). Criminals steal or fake the web domains of scholarly publishers, hijack their journals, steal the personal identities of their authors, copy their logos, and take away their article processing charges (APCs). Journal hijacking shares some features with predatory publishing: both take advantage of researchers' dire need to publish in English-language journals, exploit the gold open access (OA) model that requires APCs, fool authors with deceptive practices, and overlook publication qualities. However, hijacking has its own characteristics. It is a parasitic activity upon an established journal or publisher, stealing the latter's academic prestige in the eyes of authors and readers by abusing web technologies to engage in criminal activities.

A hijacking action is usually designed to target a legitimate journal that has been indexed by the Web of Science (WoS), Scopus, or other reputable scholarly databases with necessary academic credentials. Typically, the journal is carefully selected to be one with a low WoS Journal Impact Factor (JIF), since the hijacker is afraid that authors may be scared away by a very prestigious journal with a high JIF score, but are more comfortable with email invitations from an acceptable but still mediocre publication. Technically, a journal becomes a ripe target if it is operated by a small publisher with limited resources for sophisticated website protections, or better yet, if it has not yet created an online version of its publication.

Cyber-spoofing is motivated by the prosperity of gold OA publishing that relies on authors to pay for publishing. The OA market reached over $850 million USD in 2020, though only a little more than 30% of OA journals were fee based (Pollock, 2020). This huge cash flow is so attractive that criminals would not skip it; and it only matters when, where, and how.

DOI: 10.4324/9781003029335-6

The first detected hijacking case was in 2011. Mehrdad Jalalian, the editor-in-chief of the *Electronic Physician* journal in Iran, was the first to discover hijacked journals. He and his colleagues have been enthusiastic and productive in detecting further incidents and reporting them to the scholarly community. The list of hijacked journals compiled by Jalalian and Dadkhah (2015) contains 90 titles that they tracked down between August 2011 and June 2015, and it is one of the most comprehensive lists of this type. Dadkhah *et al.* (2016a) expanded the list to 106 journals. In the early 2010s, Jeffrey Beall also maintained a hijacked journal list which had many overlaps with the former lists. Beall may have consulted various sources, including those by Jalalian and colleagues, data from a *Science* survey (Bohannon, 2015), and input from individual commenters on scholarlyoa.org, as shown in its 19 December 2016 update under the title "Hijacked Journals." Beall's list contained 115 names before it was removed from his website in January 2017.

Tracking hijacked websites requires knowledge and skills in web technologies, as well as attention and patience. Consequently, only a few information scientists have devoted their time to these efforts, and there are a limited number of studies in the literature. As such, the number of journal and publisher victims present in the existing hijacking lists represents only the tip of the iceberg. The consequence of such criminal activities has not yet been evaluated thoroughly.

6.1 Hijacking activities

Hijacking activities are pieced together by information scientists much like a police detective does in discovering a crime, collecting evidence, and identifying suspects. Then, the suspects are indicted by the scientists, who present the issues and results of the suspects' activities in publications. What is lacking in the process is the presence of a court. However, this will not prevent scientists from exposing more hijackers' crimes to alert the academics.

6.1.1 Some hijacking cases

Although there are several hijacked journal lists, such as Abalkina's list (2020a), Beall's list, and Lukić *et al.*'s list (2014), Jalalian and coauthors are the only researchers who record their experience of hijacking discovery in detail (e.g., Jalalian, 2014; Jalalian & Dadkhah, 2015; Jalalian & Mahboobi, 2014). The description below is primarily based on their documents, unless specifically mentioned otherwise. Since hijacking activities are so heavy and complicated, only representative and clearly traced cases are introduced.

The earliest hijacking activities were discovered in late 2011. In the first couple of years, the hijackers seemed to be at the stage of learning web-spoofing techniques and accumulating experience for future attacks. Notable cases in 2011–12 include the following:

August 2011   Three journals – *Science Series Data Report, Innova Ciencia,* and *Science and Nature* – were hijacked by a person using the pseudonym Ruslan Boranbaev, who registered the fake website "sciencerecord.com" for them.

October 2011   The journal *Archives des Sciences* was hijacked by Ruslan Boranbaev, who registered the fake website "sciencesarchive.com" for it.

September 2012   Another fake website, "archiveofscience.com," was registered by Ruslan Boranbaev, also for *Archives des Sciences*.

January 2014   The domain of the website "sciencesarchive.com" was listed for sale.

August 2012   The journal *Wulfenia* was hijacked by Ruslan Boranbaev, who registered "wulfeniajournal.at" for it. The domain later went offline.

August 2012   Three days later, another hijacker using the pseudonym James Robinson registered a different domain, "wulfeniajournal.com," for *Wulfenia*. The domain later went offline.

August 2012   11 days later, Ruslan Boranbaev registered a new domain, "multidisciplinarywulfenia.org," for *Wulfenia*.

Oct 2012   Several hijacked journals, including the WoS indexed journals *Natura, Doriana,* and *Cahiers des Sciences Naturelles*, were hijacked by Ruslan Boranbaev, who registered "revistas-academicas.com" for them. He convinced WoS to link to one of the fake websites from the WoS master journal list.

In subsequent years, criminals have applied more sophisticated techniques to hijack a greater quantity of journals, improve their payment transferring methods, falsify their identities, break into the WoS listing, and even compete with each other for domain registrations. Among other actions, the success in making hyperlinks to their counterfeit websites from WoS records is especially troubling.

WoS follows a standard procedure for adding website links to its indexed journals for validation and to provide convenient access to readers. Users trust WoS, and thus trust the links to connect to reliable publications. After they click a link on WoS and navigate to a website that looks professionally designed, they have no doubt that they are working with a legitimate journal and feel comfortable about submitting their articles and paying required APCs until they eventually figure out their mistake.

During 2013–2014, journal hijacking activities became more widespread and more intricate. For instance, a Spain-based journal in the field of chemistry, *Afinidad*, was hijacked four times with four different web domains.

> November 2013 An anonymous person registered the fake domain "afinidad.org" for *Afinidad*, and used the Joomla open-source content management system to design its website. The site lasted until December 2014.
>
> January 2014 A hijacker using the pseudonym Jane Madlan registered "afinidadjournal.es" for *Afinidad*. Jalalian and Dadkhah (2015) believe Jane Madlan is actually James Robinson, the hijacker who attacked *Wulfenia* a year ago. The fake website used the Open Journal System to design its interface and manage its content.

The two hijackers operated two different fake websites for the same journal concurrently. The third and fourth counterfeit websites were then also registered by the same hijacker, James Robinson, who may simply have wanted to increase the journal's visibility.

> January 2014 The fake website "afinidadjournal.org" was registered by James Robinson two days after he registered "afinidadjournal.es" for *Afinidad*.
>
> January 2014 The fake website "bdssmgdl.org" was registered by the same hijacker two days after he registered "afinidadjournal.es" for *Afinidad*.

These examples may help illustrate the extent of hijacking threats during the short time span of several years. By 2015, Jalalian and colleagues had collected 90 hijacked journals, and Beall expanded the number to more than 100. The comments left on scholarlyoa.org under the category of "Hijacked Journals" show how Beall interacted with enthusiastic users by getting information from them, answering their questions, and helping them analyze individual cases to add new hijacked titles and remove ones that were no longer hijacked. For example, the commenter "lida farahmand azar" alone provided 14 questionable websites on Beall's blog during June 2014 and May 2015. Beall examined these websites and added five to his list. Another commenter, "Edris Merufinia," provided 61 possible fake web addresses between January 2015 and June 2015, seven of which were added to the listing by Beall.

Hijacked publishing 79

Most lists display the titles of hijacked journals, their International Standard Serial Numbers (ISSNs), and authentic web addresses side-by-side with their corresponding fake websites. Table 6.1 displays five journals selected from the list of 90 hijacked journals by Jalalian & Dadkhah. Users can easily compare the legitimate journals and their fake websites.

Hijacked journals tend to have a short lifespan to avoid legal consequences. Many fake websites are registered for one year or so, and go offline once the articles and fees of the authentic journals are taken away. For instance, of the websites of 28 hijacked journals in agricultural science listed in May 2016, only 11 sites were still in operation a year later (Bravo-Vinaja, 2017). Many counterfeit web domains are listed for sale after the hijackers no longer see profits from them, and many fake websites are redirected for other commercial uses. As a result, hijacked journal lists easily become outdated, and difficult to verify and update.

Post-2015, hijacking has carried on using the business models developed previously. Dadkhah and others are still energetically tracing cybercriminals and adopting new approaches to identify hijacked journals. They are paying more attention to developing effective strategies than recording individual activities. Therefore, few criminal cases are introduced in the literature. It becomes evident that hijackers have not only targeted small publishers, but also attacked known publishers that have established infrastructure for their online publications, and published journals in the English language. Such hijacking incidents include journals from Springer Nature, such as

Table 6.1 Examples from a hijacked journal list

Legitimate journal (ISSN), authentic website	*Hijacked journal, counterfeit website*
Afinidad (0001–9704) www.aiqs.es/catala/afinidad.asp www.raco.cat/index.php/afinidad	www.afinidad.org http://iheringiaserie.bdssmgdl.org www.afinidadjournal.es www.afinidadjournal.org
Jökull (0449–0576) http://jokulljournal.is	www.jokulljournal.com www.jkljournal.org
Philippine Scientist (0079–1466)	http://psc.tomaspubs.com
The Journal of Technology (1012340–7) http://jot.ntust.edu.tw/index.php/jot/index	www.jotechno.com
Wulfenia (1561–882X) www.landesmuseum.ktn.gv.at/ 210226w_DE.htm?seite=15	www.multidisciplinarywulfenia.org www.wulfeniajournal.com www.wulfeniajournal.at

Source: Jalalian & Dadkhah, 2015, Table 1

the *International Journal of Game Theory* and the well-known *Journal of the American Medical Association* (Dadkhah et al., 2016a; Memon, 2019). Both hijacked sites are no longer accessible. Further studies have examined cyber-attacks on journals in specific disciplines such as medical science (Dadkhah et al., 2017a) and agricultural science (Bravo-Vinaja, 2017).

The reason that hijackers use fake websites to mimic legitimate journals is to fool authors in order to intercept the payment of APCs. Hijackers use various payment methods to collect money, including wire transfers to their bank accounts, credit card swiping online, and e-currency transfers. They also develop special web portals or use third-party accounts to hide their identities.

6.1.2 Key hijackers

The descriptions in the previous section introduced only a few hijackers with their pseudonyms. These cybercriminals strive to hide their personal identities, such as their postal addresses, phone numbers, and real names. In this section, three of them are introduced, along with the evidence of their actions as tracked down through their registration information.

a) Ruslan Boranbaev

This hijacker emerged in 2011 when he registered a web domain for ten hijacked and fake journals under the title of "Science Record Journals." He probably used the template of the "Canadian Center of Science and Education," and was reported to own a Sony laptop. In addition to the early group of journals he registered, he also registered another 25 websites for his other targets. His subsequent work shows more expert and systematic actions. Below is an incomplete list of his hijacked journals.

- *Archives des Sciences*
- *Cahiers des Sciences Naturelles*
- *Ciência e Técnica Vitivinícola*
- *Doriana*
- *Innova Ciencia*
- *Jokull*
- *Natura*
- *Pensee*
- *Revista Kasmera*
- *Science and Nature*
- *Science Series Data Report*
- *Sylwan*

- *Tekstil*
- *Wulfenia*

b) James Robinson

Registered with a postal address in Dubai, UAE, James Robinson is active in the journal hijacking business. He registered himself as the publisher "Tomas Publishing" for six hijacked journals. He is believed to have launched mass journal hijacking. Among his hijacked victims, the *Journal of the American Medical Association* is a renowned one. Below is an incomplete list of his hijacked journals.

- *Africa & Latin America*
- *Agrochimica*
- *Ama: Agricultural Mechanization in Asia*
- *Azariana*
- *Cadmo*
- *Chemical Modelling*
- *Der Präparator (Praparator)*
- *Education*
- *Entomon*
- *Epistemology*
- *Fauna Rossii I Sopredel Nykh Stran*
- *Italianistica: Revista di Letteratura Italiana*
- *Journal of the American Medical Association*
- *Journal of the Balkan Tribological Association*
- *Kardiologiya*
- *Philippine Scientist*
- *Politica Economica (Journal of Economic Policy)*
- *PSR Health Research Bulletin*
- *Revue Scientifique et Technique*
- *Scientia Guaianae*
- *Systems Science*
- *Teoriiai Praktika Fizicheskoi Kul'tury*
- *Terapevticheskii Arkhiv*

c) An anonymous professor

Jalalian and Dadkhah (2015) noted an anonymous professor when they chased down cybercriminals. They believed this individual was originally from Pakistan and worked as an assistant professor in computer science and information systems in Saudi Arabia. Alongside others from Pakistan, this criminal designed counterfeit websites for a group of journals and created four fake websites for *Texas Journal of Science*. The professor had a doctoral degree from a Malaysian university, and used an HP laptop between 2013–2015 for his hijacking activities. He had been recently promoted to a managerial position at the institution where he was employed. Below is an incomplete list of the journals hijacked by him and his team members.

- *BRI's Journal of Advances in Science and Technology*
- *Journal de la Société Botanique de Genève*
- *Journal of Technology*
- *Saussurea*
- *Magnt Research Report*
- *Scientific Khyber*
- *Texas Journal of Science*

6.2 Hijacking tactics

Hijackers have adopted various strategies to steal the identity of established journals. To fool authors, they make their own websites as identical to the hijacked publications as possible. The tactics used by hijackers vary by the condition of the targets and by their level of expertise in web technology.

6.2.1 Replacing expired domains

When a web domain expires and the owner has failed to renew it for a variety of reasons, or when the owner moves to a new domain, it becomes an opportunity for somebody else to take it over and start enjoying the credit that the previous business had created. This tactic happened to be the earliest detection of hijacked publishing by Jalalian (2014) in August 2011. An expired web address "sciencerecord.com" was registered by a hijacker to create three websites for hijacked journals, e.g., *Science Series Data Report, Innova Ciencia* and *Science and Nature,* and seven fictitious journals.

Bohannon (2015) decided to run a test of such a hijacking tactic. He picked a newly expired domain "hart.hr" that belonged to Život Umjetnosti, *Journal of Contemporary Art,* which has been published for the past 50 years by the Institute of Art History in Zagreb. The publisher moved the journal to a new Web domain and notified WoS of the change. But after Bohannon registered the web address, WoS still kept the old hyperlink.

6.2.2 Snatching existing domains

Hijackers snatch existing web domains and take advantage of their established reputations legally. Bohannon (2015) introduced a hijacking instance where a biomedical publisher in the UK, Euromed Communications, found itself with a slew of complaints when angry researchers blamed it for not providing them with what they paid for. This was because the publisher started a new domain after its existing domain was taken by someone else, due to the company's delay in renewing its registration. The hijacker formatted the old domain to clone Euromed Communications' website, and started taking money from authors. In this case, the hijacker legally took the domain, so the publisher found it difficult to protect itself, other than successfully convincing WoS to change the link to the correct one. Bohannon also introduced a similar case for the journal, *Ludus Vitalis*, which is published by the Centro Lombardo Toledano in Mexico in the field of philosophy of science. The hijacker used a counterfeit website to accept submissions and charged $150 USD.

By examining a group of 24 hijacked websites, Bohannon (2015) found that most of the sites have been used for different purposes:

1. For non-publishing businesses. For example, two counterfeit websites are now used for hair-loss cures and payday loans, while the original domains were created for the *Journal of Plant Biotechnology*, the product of a Korean scholarly society, and *Graphis Scripta*, a botany journal published by the Nordic Lichen Society. The hijackers only want to benefit from traffic to these websites.
2. For unknown use. For example, the web address for a group of seven University of Liverpool journals was snatched to host a site that promotes manuscript submissions with only a generic "contact" button.
3. For sale. For example, a domain for *Lankesteriana*, a plant science journal published by the University of Costa Rica, now has a link to a private auction to sell the domain.

6.2.3 Taking advantage of print journals

In many cases, print journals are the targets of hijacking. Butler (2013) reported two incidents where hijackers designed counterfeit websites for print-only legitimate journals to defraud authors for APCs. One is *Archives des Sciences*, a journal launched in 1791 in Switzerland, and the other is *Wulfenia*, a botany journal published in Austria. These counterfeit websites pretended to represent the authentic journals by including the titles of the journals, their JIFs, addresses, and ISSNs. Their pages were designed so well that even WoS agreed to include a link to one of the journals, causing confusion among authors and readers.

Fortunately, WoS removed the link immediately after detecting a discrepancy in the number of the journal issues between its print version and its fake website. However, the damage to the authentic journal was serious and long lasting. Because each fake website asks for an APC of $500 USD, researchers who paid the APCs but did not see their articles in the print journal complained to the authentic journals.

The real journals reported the crimes to their respective authorities, the Cybercrime Coordination Unit Switzerland and Austrian police. However, the counterfeit domain of *Archives des Sciences* was found to be hosted in the US rather than in Switzerland, and the fake *Wulfenia* website have multiple replicas on servers in other countries, which is beyond the control of Austrian police. Both journals started developing their own online versions after the hijacking incidents.

After analyzing more cases of this type, Jalalian and Mahboobi (2014) found the victimized print-only journals all: (i) were published by small publishers, (ii) had low WoS JIF values that could more realistically draw in submissions, and (iii) were based in non-English-speaking countries where the identity of the hijackers could easily be hidden. The counterfeit websites were usually designed with a professional look. The hijackers then marketed on behalf of the original journals by indicating the journals' WoS JIFs, and by applying deceptive strategies similar to what predatory journals have used.

6.2.4 Tricking users with similar domains

One easy form of journal hijacking is to construct a similar domain address and website, enticing authors to submit papers as if they were submitting to the real journal. Bohannon (2015) specified that the web domain of *Science Magazine* (sciencemag.org) was mimicked by someone who registered sciencmag.org and drove web traffic to the cloned website. Careless authors might not pay attention to the difference between these two web addresses: one omits an "e" intentionally.

An unfortunate victim is *Sylwan*, a journal in the field of forestry published by the Polish Forestry Society (Lukić *et al.*, 2014). It has earned its reputation as one of the oldest academic journals since its creation in 1820. The domain of the journal was hijacked and presented as the English edition of the Polish journal (Figure 6.1). In order to make the counterfeit website look legitimate, the hijacker even edited the Wikipedia article about the journal, and inserted its own web address and a call for papers into the

Hijacked publishing 85

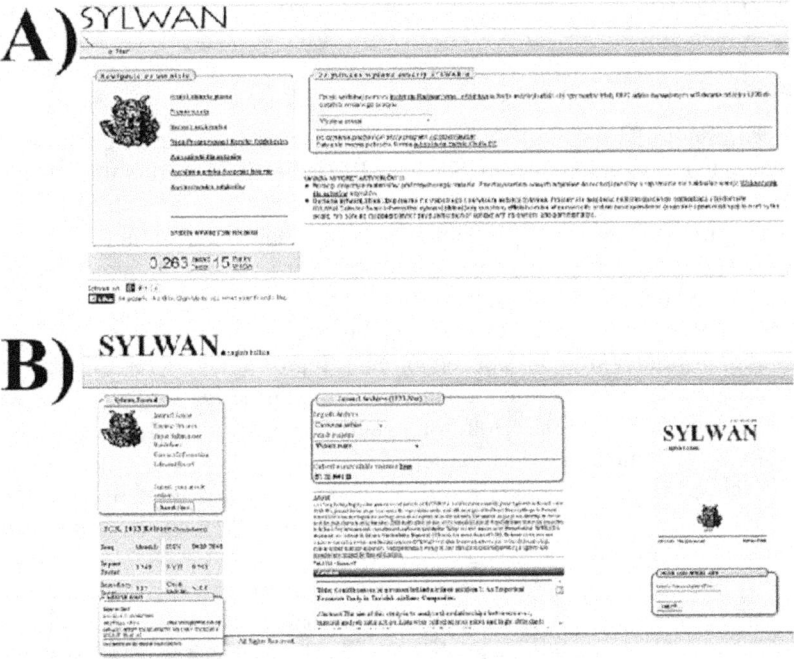

Figure 6.1 Website of the legitimate journal *Sylwan* (A) and its hijacked English version (B)

Source: Lukić *et al.*, 2014, Figure 2

Wikipedia article. It is thus difficult for even experienced authors to realize the difference between the real journal and the fake one.

In addition to the hijacking methods described here, information scientists have also attempted to figure out other potential hijacking tactics so as to better understand hijacking behaviors. Dadkhah *et al.* (2017a) tested SEO (search engine optimization) techniques and found them to be an effective strategy to enhance traffic. Using UlrichWeb, one of the most comprehensive journal indexes in the world, they searched suspended journals and designed new websites by copying the journals' titles. Next, the scientists created a second website for each of the suspended journals, and used SEO to optimize the visibility of the second websites in search engines. With the SEO technique, these websites were returned in the first eight search results. The scientists continued examining existing hijacked websites, and found that most were returned in the first or second page of their search results

86 Hijacked publishing

on search engines. Hence, they suggested that journals with weak SEO are most vulnerable to journal hijacking.

6.3 Detecting hijacking

According to Bohannon (2015), because the targets of hijacking activities are primarily legitimate journals with a JIF score, the detection of hijacked journals can begin with the WoS journal master records. In the records, the information of roughly 21,500 journals is searchable, including their titles, ISSNs, subject categories, JIF values, and their web and postal addresses. Starting with these web addresses will effectively limit the extent of a search and make the discovery of hijacked journals more focused. Scopus provides similar information for its indexed journals. Figure 6.2 is a screenshot of the journal *Afinidad*, indexed in Scopus through its free web service SCImago Journal & Country Rank. Both the hyperlink to this journal and its email address are at the lower right corner.

With a list of web addresses of the WoS or Scopus journals, one can search their domain registration data through the WHOIS directory. The Internet Corporation for Assigned Names and Numbers, which is responsible for coordinating the namespaces and numerical spaces of the Internet, requires all domain name registrars to provide their contact information and store the information on the WHOIS database, which is publicly available. One can check if the registration data is recent, which is suspicious if the journal has been in operation for a long time. This would be the first clue which might encourage a researcher to further investigate whether the domain's country of registration matches the country of the publisher.

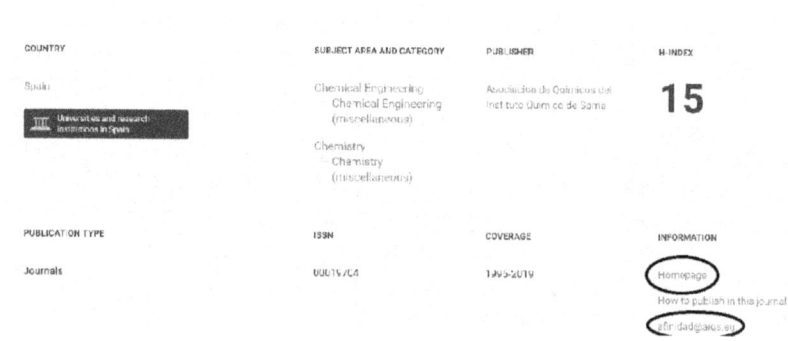

Figure 6.2 The journal *Afinidad* and its information, available on SCImago

The researcher can then verify if the publisher's name and contact information are anonymous, and the domain was purchased through a private domain registrar. Therefore, the registration date provides useful information about journals with recently-changed web domains, and the researcher can then examine the individual websites.

Using this technique, the aforementioned Iranian scientists have been able to locate many hijacked journals. Bohannon (2015) followed the same path to detect 24 journals indexed by WoS whose web addresses appear to have been recently snatched. He called for WoS to remain careful with verifying and maintaining the validity of journal hyperlinks.

Dadkhah *et al.* (2016b) adopted a different approach to identify hijacked journals and prevent the indexing of articles in these journals by respected citation databases. Upon analyzing known hijacked journals, they classified 12 features to identify hijacking (see Table 6.2). These features can be searched, verified, calculated, and compared through web tools such as Google, WHOIS, the Alexa database, and a data mining tool WEKA that includes machine learning algorithms. Each feature will be calculated for a value and the sum of the values will be interpreted into patterns for identifying hijacking. In the calculations, some fancy algorithms are applied to extract a decision tree which is then used to "write full rules for detecting hijacked journals" (Dadkhah *et al.*, 2016b, p. 302).

Table 6.2 Features to identify hijacked journals

Feature	Method of Calculation
Page Rank	Extracted from Google Page Rank algorithm
Number of External links	Counted by number of website's source code links
Domain lifetime	Searched on WHOIS for times of journal's URL
Indexing	Mentioned for indexing on WoS or Scopus
Sequence in searching results	Returned by Google for times of website's title
Visitor's country	Found from Alexa for country of journal visitors
Availability of previous issues	Based on availability of all issues on website
Long URL	Counted by length of website's address
Aim and Scope	Calculated by number of subjects of publications
Link in databases	Counted by links in scientific databases
Full text	Checked if full text is available for publications
Author's country	Checked by text mining journal's website & its papers

Source: Dadkhah *et al.*, 2016b, Table 1

Journal hijacking is considered to use similar techniques as web phishing (Dadkhah *et al.*, 2015). Like journal hijacking, phishing is conducted by attackers to direct victims to counterfeit websites using social engineering techniques. Unlike journal hijacking, phishing attacks not only target academic authors, but also other types of users. Yet, when phishing scams go after journals, they yield very similar results to journal hijacking. Dadkhah *et al.* (2015) introduced a method based on classification algorithms to identify journal phishing attacks and tested the method against a group of known phished journals. The same approach was also used to compare a group of authentic and hijacked journals for the same purpose (Shahri *et al.*, 2018).

6.4 Hijacked articles

Major citation databases like WoS and Scopus have implemented an evaluation process and well-tested selection criteria to block fake publications. For example, WoS uses expert in-house editors to review and determine the inclusion of journals in its core databases. The editors have no affiliations with publishing houses or research institutes, and they focus on specific subject fields with a deep, nuanced knowledge of the journals in relevant fields. They apply a set of 28 criteria to evaluate journals for publication quality and best practices. Scopus has a similar publication selection mechanism, but also emphasizes its continuous review process to make sure publications continuously meet the rigorous requirements of scholarly publishing.

In theory, these databases have the capability to filter out publications in hijacked journals that do not follow professional standards and present low to no academic quality in their content. Unfortunately, the reality is quite the opposite. Cybercriminals seem to have been able to penetrate the rigorous reviews and establish themselves in most citation databases. Dadkhah *et al.* (2017b) ran a test using the "Publish or Perish" application, developed by a management professor in the UK, to discover papers published in hijacked journals through database search engines. They conducted the search against the titles from Beall's hijacked journal list and found a great number of indexed papers, e.g., a total of 218 papers in the journal *Ayer* were detected through its fake website ayeronline.com; the number of papers was 181 for *MULTITEMAS* on its website multitemas.com/index.php/MTJournal and 46 for *Academie Royal des Sciences d Outre-Mer Bulletin des Seances* on the counterfeit website ardsj.com (Dadkhah *et al.*, 2017b, p. 183).

Another study of the cloned website for the journal *Talent Development and Excellence* found that the hijacker successfully listed nearly 500 articles in the Scopus database in 2020 (Abalkina, 2020b; see also Al-Amr, 2020). Although Scopus removed the publications from its index after complaints from the authentic journal, the effectiveness of journal hijacking is evident.

Hijacked journals often steal articles from legitimate journals or even predatory journals. For example, it was found recently that most of the content in *Biochemia Medica* has been copied illegally by some hijacked journals (Memon, 2019). This is the official journal of the Croatian Society of Medical Biochemistry and Laboratory Medicine, which is published in English and does not ask for APCs. Abalkina (2020a) believes that the hijackers want to fool authors with the legitimacy of their journals by presenting them with archived text. In practice, anything published in hijacked journals may become "lost science" because of the short lifespan of most hijacked websites.

The number of authors who publish in hijacked journals is by no means small. When forgers have mimicked the website of a legitimate journal and successfully cheated authors, they will inevitably seek to publish all submissions to maximize profit, regardless of the quality and suitability of the submissions. Unlike many predatory publishers, who may have a relatively long-term plan (or at least they hope so), hijacked journals are mostly short-lived, with a grab-and-run approach. There is no study so far to calculate how many authors have published in hijacked journals and how many such articles have been made available, due to limited studies on this subject. But Dadkhah and Borchardt's count (2016, p. 740) of only 10 hijacked journals yielded as many as 2,442 papers during the first five months of 2015, suggesting a large quantity of hijacked publications in existence. Dadkhah *et al.* (2016a) found that some hijacked journals could publish as many as 1,500 papers per issue. When a call for papers comes from a journal which has a genuine JIF and is indeed indexed by reputable databases, authors tend to welcome the opportunity, because they do not know the call is actually from a hijacker. This is different from a predatory journal that is using fake JIFs and can only fool inexperienced authors. Therefore, Jalalian and Dadkhah (2015) suggested that the academic community give authors who publish in hijacked journals a second chance to publish their papers in legitimate journals.

6.5 Conclusion

By all accounts, hijacked publishing has created a real challenge for scholarly publishing. It is unfortunate that academics have not been completely aware of the practices and the dangers of hijacked publishing as they have been with predatory publishing (Memon, 2019). Hijacked publications may have a short life in most cases, but journal hijacking activities can be a long-term phenomenon. The hijacking techniques introduced in this chapter include those that have already been used by cybercriminals and those that are hypothesized and tested by information scientists who are investigating the subject. However, because hijackers always try to explore and adopt new tactics, the fight against such crime will be a constant one.

7 Conferences

This chapter introduces the details of predatory conferences and provides resources to assist researchers in identifying such activities. It describes how, over the years, predatory conferences have become a lucrative business for predators to expand their revenue, how the business has changed the behavior of many academics and professionals in scientific pursuits, and how individual efforts have been made to expose the misconduct of predatory conferences.

7.1 Background

Academic conferences provide opportunities for researchers, within academia and beyond, to present and discuss their studies, or to listen to others' discoveries at the frontiers of science, and gain knowledge in particular topics. These are also networking events for researchers to seek collaborations, or simply socialize with colleagues or acquaintances whom they may see once a year or even less. Many academic conferences publish their presentations and posters upon acceptance, free of charge, in proceedings. In some disciplines, reputable conference proceedings have a greater scholarly value than journal papers.

Conferences have become an integral part of academic life for most, if not all, scholars, much like scholarly journals. Predators who exploit journal publishing see conferences as another avenue to gain revenue. Predatory conferencing became a lucrative industry even earlier than predatory publishing has been in practice, and has developed into a more profitable business than the latter. Imitating legitimate events, predatory organizers take various types of meeting structures such as conferences, workshops, symposia, trade shows, exhibitions, and science congresses in almost all academic subjects, across different regions, and in both physical and virtual formats of delivery. Their predatory conduct has tellingly penetrated every

DOI: 10.4324/9781003029335-7

academic pursuit's dissemination of scholarship, and will remain active so long as the business proves lucrative.

7.2 Characteristics of predatory conferences

Suspicious conferences were detected as early as 2002 (Cohen, 2013). Jeffrey Beall featured what he called "predatory meetings" when he posted them on his website in January 2013. He introduced the OMICS International (OMICS), and listed some major characteristics of its operations. He periodically introduced new findings, but never developed a comprehensive list of predatory conferences. Others have attempted to provide a list of the predatory conferences they have identified (e.g., Cobey *at al.*, 2017; Cress, 2017). However, none of their lists are comprehensive enough or updated frequently enough to cover the major predatory activities of identified organizers, conferences, and related events.

Beall observed three pieces of evidence for early predatory meetings: (i) they used the names of scholars on the conference websites or in invitation letters without consulting them, (ii) they made their conference names similar to existing, recognized meetings, and (iii) they refused to refund registration fees when their conferences were cancelled. For instance, before the Entomological Society of America held its annual International *Congress* of Entomology in 2013, OMICS called for participation in its International *Conference* of Entomology. The former adopted "Entomology 2013" as its acronym, while OMICS shortened its own conference to "Entomology-2013" with a hyphen (Kolata, 2013).

McCrostie (2020) identified three major characteristics of predatory conferences: (i) those that provide low-quality academic meetings exclusively for a profit, (ii) those that do not provide peer review as claimed, but allow everyone to purchase a speaking slot, and (iii) those that use deceitful tactics in almost all aspects of operations to entice participants.

Predatory conferences are complex in practice and vary considerably by many factors. There are no industrial standards and professional regulations in predatory conferences, although individual studies have discussed criteria or signs to identify them (e.g., Asadi *et al.*, 2017). This chapter provides only summarized descriptions from a small part of the literature.

7.2.1 Criteria to identify predatory conferences

Researchers have recommended that the standards of academic conferences should include codes of conduct and quality control policies (e.g., Foxx *et al.*, 2019), particularly the quality of proceedings in technical conferences (Kulamer *et al.*, 2017). Of those who have addressed the nuisance of predatory conferences, Memon and Azim (2018) and McCrostie (2017) provide some of the most extensive measures, although their measures are only based on personal observations and have not been connected to any list of historical and existing predatory conferences.

Table 7.1 is a compilation of several sets of criteria developed by previous studies. Many measures are similar to those used to identify predatory

Table 7.1 List of indicators of predatory conferences

Evidence of deceitful practices
Novices are invited to be keynote speakers
A for-profit conference organizer claims to be not-for-profit
Advisory boards or organizing committees contain names who are not consulted
Falsely claims universities or organizations as partners or sponsors
Spam emails are regularly sent to people outside the field of the conference
Email invitations contain language problems and use free email accounts
Email invitations contain flattery, specific references to the recipient's work
Provides incorrect addresses or contact numbers
Provides incorrect locations of operations
Provides no or wrong information about the real organizers
Evidence of falsified peer review
No peer review exists, or single-reader review of submissions
Reviews are taken only by conference organizers or owners
Peer reviewers, if they exist, do not have subject expertise
Vetting of peer reviewers is absent or inadequate
Evidence of high fees
Registration fee is higher than typical in the field
Presenters pay more than attendees
No refund policy is presented
Refunds are not provided even if the organizers cancel a conference
Fees are transferred through Western Union or to personal bank accounts
Evidence of predatory naming conventions
Names of conferences match the names of established conferences
Names are labeled *international, world*, or *global*, but country-bound
Names are labeled *international, world*, or *global*, but very few attendees
Evidence of broad scope
Organizers simultaneously hold many meetings at the same time and hotel
Same conference is held multiple times a year in different cities
Single organizer plans conferences in very different academic fields
Conferences have a wide-ranging focus with vague objectives
Evidence of fast acceptance
Submitted abstracts or papers are accepted within a week, if not a day
Submitted abstracts or papers are accepted before the deadline of Call for Papers
Submissions are allowed after the deadline of Call for Papers
Abstract submission guidelines are missing or ambiguous
Evidence of unprofessional conduct in virtual presentations

(*Continued*)

94 Conferences

Table 7.1 (Continued)

Accepted papers are not presented to audience
Virtual presentations published in proceedings are not identified as such
Evidence of misinformation on publications
Falsely claims to publish papers in journals of WoS, Scopus or other indexing
No plan to digitally preserve proceedings and make them accessible
Conference papers get funneled to known or suspended predatory journals
Evidence of irregular operations
Conferences get regularly cancelled or changed on short notice
Conference dinners or associated tours are offered at a profit
Presenters, session chairs, or proceeding editors have ties to other predatory events
Best paper prizes are awarded before the end of conference
Multiple best papers are awarded

journals, which make sense since they are all predatory in nature and some share the same managers and owners. Since the measures are observation-based, they reflect the actual practices of predatory conferencing. By examining these features, one will be able to imagine what a predatory conference may look like. Note that this is not a commonly agreed-upon list of criteria, and cannot cover the entirety or complexity of predatory conference practices.

7.2.2 Scale of predatory conferencing

The predatory conference market has expanded exponentially in the past decades, although there are no studies examining its exact size and profitability. Simply looking at the magnitude of some well-known parasitic conference giants, such as OMICS, one can tell how financially successful their business has been. To better understand the dimensions and scope of the industry, some examples are introduced below.

OMICS is a major event empire that provides more than 3,000 meetings annually through its Conference Series LLC LTD, including over 1,000 conferences, over 1,000 symposiums, and more than 1,000 workshops. Their subject coverage includes biomedicine, pharmaceutical science, engineering, natural science, technology, and business management. Their conferences are held mostly in attractive locations across Europe, Asia, Australia, New Zealand, Canada, and Brazil. Because of COVID-19, nearly half of its planned 1,200 events were moved online in 2021. From the beginning of its service in 2008 to early 2021, OMICS organized a huge number of conference-related events and made large profits. The company claimed to receive $11.6 million USD in its 2016 revenue. The cost to attend most of its conferences is more than $1,000 USD. In April 2019, the US Federal Trade Commission announced that the federal district court ordered OMICS "to pay more than $50.1 million to resolve ... a 2016 Commission complaint" that alleged OMICS "falsely advertised online scientific and medical academic journals and international conferences, and deceptively claimed the journals provided authors with rigorous peer review and editorial boards comprised of prominent academics" (Federal Trade Commission, 2019).

The World Academy of Science, Engineering and Technology (WASET) is another giant conference organizer that serves all academic subjects. It was listed as a predatory publisher by Beall and subsequently listed by predatoryjournals.com. WASET listed around 310 locations of planned conferences from April 2021 to December 2022 on its website, all in large cities or tourist spots. Each location has an excessive number of conferences. For example, in Cancun, Mexico, there were as many as 2,170 different conferences scheduled on 5–6 April 2021 alone, each of which charged €400 ($470 USD) as the standard registration. An earlier study by Eckert *et al.* (2018) found that WASET organized 53,478 conferences in 2018, with an estimated revenue of $4,495,219 USD. This is a conservative estimate, given the total number of its complete conferences.

The International Congress and Convention Association (ICCA) compiled a long list with nearly 100 predatory conference organizers, but the list is accessible only to its members (McMillin, 2019). The Kscien Organization (2021) in Kurdistan, Iraq, maintained a list of 467 individual predatory conferences as of April 2021. But none of these, or other lists, is as comprehensive due to the complexity of the industry. An unconfirmed report on the scope of predatory conferences estimates that such conferences had already outnumbered legitimate scholarly events by 2017 (Grove, 2017).

7.3 Stakeholders

7.3.1 Some conference organizers

As described previously, OMICS was founded and managed by a young man who received his PhD from an Indian university and spent three months as a postdoctoral student at Stanford University. He describes his motivation of creating the publishing and conferencing business as being to provide everyone with open access to scholarly materials that are otherwise unavailable to people who cannot afford them. For OMICS products, he claims to have provided, or is striving to provide, the highest level of quality control, although the majority of those who have experience with his activities disagree with his claims (Deprez & Chen, 2017).

The owners of WASET were tracked down by three European journalists who investigated its web domain through WHOIS (Eckert et al., 2018; Oberhaus, 2018). These journalists found connections between the domain and 83 other domain names, and discovered a Turkish family behind this business. According to their evidence, WASET is registered in Azerbaijan and maintained in Turkey by a man, his daughter, and his son since 2007.

Most predatory organizers hide their identities and constantly change their websites and names to escape the predatory label (McCrostie, 2020). Extra steps are needed to explore their ownership and relationship with other entities. For example, OMICS changed the brand of its conference branch to several different names after the US federal court ruled in FTC's favor against it. McCrostie (2016) found the International Business Academics Consortium partnered with three other conference organizers and shared some advisory members, and the Higher Education Forum connects itself to another company. These organizers were found to have substantial educational backgrounds and to understand the infrastructure and process of, as well as demands in, scholarship dissemination.

7.3.2 Keynotes, planning committee members, and attendees

Predatory conferences typically claim that their keynote speakers consist of world-renowned scientists in relevant academic fields, including Nobel laureates. Recognized researchers appear frequently on the list of the conferences' panels and organizing or review committees (e.g., Ruben, 2016). Some distinguished scholars may have indeed participated in events offered by predatory organizers and left with a pleasant experience (Cohen, 2013), probably because the organizers know the market value of the superstars and made special arrangements for them. Their names will be used extensively for future promotions. However, these are only a minority of cases, and those presenting at the conferences and serving as committee members are extensively reported to be unsatisfied. For example:

- A UK-based researcher found the conference he spoke at was full of Taiwanese graduate students who were not interested in his presentation (McCrostie, 2016). To graduate in Taiwan, students are required to attend international conferences and are provided with about $1,265 USD by the government if they present there. Many take advantage of predatory conferences' easy acceptance.
- A journalist going to an OMICS-run conference to investigate predatory activities found a renowned Japanese professor giving a plenary speech, but leaving after his presentation (Mackenzie, 2019). Then, "things started to get a little weird" – many speakers did not show up;

the topics smashed together to provide a loosely connected talk series; and the session chair and committee members had no control over the meeting agenda or were disconnected from each other.
- A practicing scientist found his colleague on a list of distinguished speakers and as the chair of a session by a conference (Ruben, 2016). The colleague actually only replied to an earlier invitation to ask if his travel costs would be paid. This simple reply gave the conference provider an excuse to list his name. Although this colleague asked his name to be removed, his request was completely ignored.
- The conference organizer, Eureka Science, listed a handful of Nobel Laureates on many of its conference keynote speaker lists. For example, the co-winner of the 1998 Nobel Prize in Physiology or Medicine, Ferid Murad, was listed as the president for at least three of its conferences in 2016 and a keynote speaker for other conferences (Ika, 2015).
- The Research Chair at the North York General Hospital in Canada, who is also affiliated with the University of Toronto, was listed as the featured speaker at a nursing international conference without her consent (Fedele, 2019).

Reports reveal that identity theft is common. Predatory conferences post the photos and bios of renowned scholars on their websites and list them as keynote speakers or members of committees without their consent (Pai & Franco, 2016). The Royal Society of Chemistry (RSC) events and exhibitions manager estimates that in the chemistry sector alone, there are "hundreds, if not thousands" of counterfeit conferences with potentially illegitimate uses of members of the RSC community, and "most of the time, they're completely unaware that their name is being used to promote a fake event" (McMillin, 2019). McGill University discovered that 220 of its professors were listed as "editors, contributors and speakers" for OMICS conferences, which these professors did not have knowledge of (Gillis, 2018). In fact, OMICS has claimed many more academics in Canada on its conference websites, including 314 names from the University of Toronto, 253 from York University, 182 from the University of Alberta, 59 from Dalhousie University, and 38 from Concordia University (Gillis, 2018).

Scholars may be flattered when receiving email invitations to give keynote speeches at self-proclaimed "international" conferences. Such invitations are especially attractive to many junior scholars who are in dire need of venues to establish their academic reputations (Mercier *et al.*, 2018). They may not know the difference between a predatory conference and a legitimate one (Ruben, 2016), but are interested in taking any possible opportunity to add to their CVs and have fun traveling to exotic destinations. Many academics who receive the invitations may harbor suspicions as a result of the mismatch between the conference themes and their own research areas, but since many predatory conferences have a broad coverage of subjects, some invitees may never pay attention to the differences.

Not everyone is an unfortunate victim; many are knowing participants. The easy acceptance to predatory conferences provides people with possibilities to amplify their credentials (Brooks, 2009). Many institutions have a policy of compensating those who can present evidence of an invitation to speak at international or national conferences (e.g., McCrostie, 2016). At predatory conferences, all attendees can be speakers if they are willing to pay for it. These academics may be aware of the nature of the conferences but decide to take advantage of them for various reasons. They do not take these opportunities as seriously, which explains why many conference attendees register but do not attend, or attend but do not stay, e.g., "a scientist who had traveled to a genetic engineering conference only to find a total of 19 attendees, half of whom disappeared by the second day" (Ruben, 2016). This represents a popular pattern with predatory conferences.

McCrostie (2020) has a pessimistic view of the attitudes and behaviors of individual scholars and institutions when it comes to accepting and cooperating with predatory conferences. He uses examples to show the willingness of some academics to speak at predatory events, and their continuous services and defense of these meetings even after they become aware of the unethical practices of the organizers. He also points to the tolerance of some universities in allowing organizers to rent their facilities for bogus activities, citing the University of Cambridge and Oxford University as examples. Nonetheless, the literature describes more cases wherein scholars are cheated than cases of willing participation in such activities.

7.3.3 Conference publications

Predatory conferences promise to publish abstracts or short papers that individuals present or post at meetings. When conference organizers are also publishers themselves, they tend to publish papers in proceedings or in special issues of regular journals. When they are not, they usually funnel papers to collaborating predatory journals. Since predatory conferences accept all applications without providing peer review, the quality of the publications tends to fluctuate from very few good ones by innocent attendees, to an overwhelming majority of mediocre ones by knowing participants.

Some European journalists decided to examine conference publications available online (Oberhaus, 2018). They filtered out tens of thousands of proceedings abstracts on the OMICS and WASET websites, of which roughly 15,000 are by individuals from India, and around 10,000 are contributed by scholars from the US. These journalists then analyzed authors' affiliations of the publications, and realized that these

> range from academics trying to boost their publishing profile to scientists affiliated with companies who want to boost their scientific cred by having some publications under their belt. A distressing number of these academics come from elite American universities, as well. Eckert and her colleagues discovered 162 papers submitted to WASET and OMICS journals from Stanford, 153 papers from Yale, 96 from Columbia, and 94 from Harvard in the last decade . . . this goes way beyond academia.
>
> (Oberhaus, 2018)

7.4 Predatory medical conferences

Many major corporations are active participants and even help predatory publishers organize, broadcast, and host conferences. Chapman (2016) reported that the tobacco company Philip Morris promoted on its website the 3rd International Conference on Chronic Obstructive Pulmonary Disease in Brisbane, Australia. This is a conference organized by OMICS.

Pharmaceutical science is the epicenter of predatory conferences. Drug companies see their names frequently on the supporting and participating list of predatory conferences by OMICS and other organizers. It remains unknown if they are aware of the reputations of these conferences, but the fact that almost all pharmaceutical giants in the West are involved in the business indicate possible correlations, although there is no direct evidence (Deprez & Chen, 2017).

Indirect evidence, on the other hand, does reveal poorly conducted studies in predatory publications by some of the companies. It is also unclear if these predatory publications and conference connections represent individuals' selections or corporations' behaviors. At the very least, these companies have not developed any mechanisms to prevent their sponsored clinical research from skirting rigorous peer review and presenting at low-quality, questionable conferences. Because pharmaceutical companies tend to communicate their discoveries to doctors and other medical practitioners, their connections to predatory conferences are very concerning.

OMICS admits that around 60% of its revenue comes from pharmaceutical companies that sponsor its conferences and send their researchers to present at the meetings (Deprez & Chen, 2017). Many companies lead workshops at OMICS's conferences, and speakers are often from these companies. When they were contacted, they either refused to answer questions or defended their publishing policies. However, many companies claimed to continuously strengthen their staff training programs, improve their communication policies, and enhance their research agenda.

The penetration rate of predatory conferences into the health care profession, including pharmaceutical science, has been more obvious than other professions. This explains why most editorial pieces, commentaries, and scientific investigations about predatory practices are published by health professionals and scholars (Mertkan *et al.*, 2021). Many doctors and practitioners are relatively inexperienced or very busy when it comes to identifying predatory journals and conferences, and therefore may potentially incorporate research results from these venues into their practices, which can be disastrous.

7.5 Combatting predatory conferences

7.5.1 Sting operations

Many researchers fall prey to spam invitations and learn the hard way from their experiences. Some have decided to plan sting operations. McCrostie (2016) used SCIgen to create grammatically correct but nonsensical papers, and submitted them to conferences operated by two Taiwan-based organizers. All submissions were accepted by the organizers, who claimed to have conducted rigorous peer review through at least two reviewers. Each organizer asked the author to pay a fee up to $450 USD for registration, but they all refused to answer the author's questions when he pointed out the gibberish of his papers and asked questions about how they spent their income. Using one of the conferences as an example to calculate the revenue, McCrostie counted 300 attendees, multiplied the figure by $400 USD for each registration, and arrived at $120,000 USD in revenue. He then checked with the conference local chair to discover very minimal overhead: only four classrooms were rented at a university. McCrostie attended one conference and found it accommodated four meetings covering completely different topics (McMillin, 2019). During the conference, he observed absent presenters and found many presenters left early for a local tour.

Another sting operation was undertaken by Eckert *et al.* (2018) against WASET. They travelled to a WASET event in London and found it lasted only two hours with a half-dozen attendees in a small room. Another university professor in New Zealand used his phone's autocomplete feature to generate a meaningless paper and submitted it to an OMICS event, International Conference on Atomic and Nuclear Physics, with a fake name and employment affiliation (Bartneck, 2016). Only three hours later, his submission was accepted. In response to his queries about the quick acceptance,

OMICS explained that the paper slipped through due to the closeness of the submission to the conference's deadline.

Heasman (2019) carried out another sting operation. Upon receiving many unsolicited invitations, he looked at the organizing committee members of several conferences and contacted them for answers. Since those who replied to his queries all denied their connections to the meetings, he decided to visit one of the organizers whose address was listed in a nearby city. The address, however, was a sandwich shop. To test for the existence of any peer review by the conferences, he then created a fake paper with grammatical and technical errors, unrelated title and content, and absurd narrative, and expected it to be accepted. He was not disappointed. He then paid €680 ($814 USD) and attended one conference, only to find out that all the organizing committee members were absent, and there were only about ten attendees crammed in a small room, which was adjacent to two other small rooms for different conferences (Heasman, 2019). His conference did not have sponsors or exhibitors, only four posters were displayed, and at least one speaker did not attend to present. Overall, the experience was awful.

7.5.2 Actions by the conference industry

The rapid expansion of predatory conferences has created real damage to the conducting of research. These conferences are not only threatening the academic system, but have also become a problem for the meeting industry. The ICCA CEO states that these conferences present "an industrial-scale challenge to bonafide associations and their quality education programs" (McMillin, 2019). Their aggressive and unethical behaviors have brought tremendous competition to the conference playing field, and at the same time have jeopardized the industry's hard-won reputation.

Professionals find it hard to stop predatory conferences because legal actions may not be practicable. Attempts to issue cease-and-desist letters do not seem to be effective enough to prevent fake conference activities. Many legitimate organizers budget extra money to block housing space, but find it to not be a valid strategy. The ICCA has developed a list containing predatory conference organizers and asks its members to check space requests against the list to decide whether to host certain events. The list has nearly 100 suspicious conference organizers and is available only to ICCA members.

The conference industry has recognized the significance of promoting awareness among individual organizers. Many have worked together to develop guidelines, identify fraudulent events, and evaluate potential threats. Some ideas have been developed to combat predatory conferences, such as creating a recognition mechanism with a vetting process to demonstrate the legitimacy of an organizer (McMillin, 2019). Overall, it will be a joint effort for the industry to collaborate with professional associations and individual researchers in the academic community and beyond to protect the business.

The academic community has also developed strategies to combat predatory practices. In addition to promoting awareness, other initiatives have been taken individually. For example, McGill University's faculty of medicine decided to adjust its policies by making a clear statement in all letters of appointment and reappointment, and planning to extend it to the whole university:

> Research findings and other scholarly contributions should be published only in well-established and credible scientific journals that employ rigorous peer review. Similarly, engagement in and attendance at conferences where your research results are presented, as well as your service in editorial boards, must reflect the same high standards of academic integrity.
>
> (Gillis, 2018)

7.6 How to avoid predatory conferences

Lang *et al.* (2019) conducted surveys among medical faculty and residents and found that faculty select conferences for their topics, plenary speakers, and cutting-edge research, while medical residents care about the topics, opportunity to present own work, and recommendations from others. These findings correspond to the popular opinion and discoveries that young researchers are the most vulnerable targets of predatory conferences. They also found that established scholars are more likely to receive email spam (71%), compared to around 56% for the residents. Given the fact that junior researchers tend to listen to mentors and peers about conferences, it is necessary to target this group to improve their knowledge and guide them through the selection process.

Inspired by Think.Check.Submit, Think.Check.Attend (Figure 7.1) was initiated in 2018 to provide step-by-step guides for researchers to check appropriate conferences before submitting an abstract and agreeing to attend. It is based in the UAE and created by Knowledge E, an information and service provider, that encourages academics to utilize the service for conference credentials. In guiding users through the process, the "think" function is for users to think through current issues posed by predatory and substandard conferences, the "check" function suggests that users examine criteria that help differentiate questionable conferences from legitimate ones, and the "attend" function ensures trusted conferences are evaluated and confirmed.

Figure 7.1 Logo of Think.Check.Attend
Source: With permission from Knowledge E

The theory behind this initiative is that a blacklist will be unable to capture the complexity of predatory conferences, let alone the absence of any comprehensive meeting blacklists. Even blacklists themselves face constant criticism of the accuracy of their inclusions. The best strategy to fight dishonorable academic activities is to educate individual researchers about how to identify appropriate practices themselves. Tools developed by the initiative can serve as self-training opportunities to educate individuals about how to avoid falling prey to bogus conferences.

7.7 Conclusion

In the discussion of predatory conferences, there are more media and newspaper reports than scientific studies. The reports tell stories of fraudulent marketing, identity theft, disorganized events, tiny attendance, expensive registration fees, mediocre publications, and much more. Many readers leave comments to express their anger at engaging with the conferences or describe their unique experiences. Reading the reports and comments helps understand the threat of predatory conferences to scholarly culture. This chapter selects only a small part of these materials. Most scholarly publications are in the form of editorials, commentaries, and opinions. Very few scientific investigations have been undertaken to explore predatory conferences (Nisha *et al.*, 2020). Criteria for identifying predatory events are piecemeal and controversial to some extent.

The major concern about predatory conferences is the participation in, and support from, major pharmaceutical companies that use predatory events as regular venues to communicate their research results. It does not only erode public trust in legitimate research, but also poses an existential threat to clinical studies, with potentially dangerous impacts on medical practices. Scholars need to collaborate with policymakers, practitioners, publishers, and the public to explore the ecosystem and practices of predatory conferencing and develop workable strategies to fight against these predatory behaviors.

The online delivery of conferences has provided new opportunities for predatory organizers. Organizers have all adjusted their delivery methods and started taking various virtual formats. The impact of online meetings on the predatory business is still unknown. However, predators will mutate their approaches to adopt to the changing environment, and will continuously bring fresh challenges to the scholarly community and beyond.

8 Metrics and indexes

Unlike the popular Journal Impact Factors (JIF) by the Web of Science (WoS), predatory metrics are unreproducible and based on unreliable or opaque criteria. At the same time, there are open access (OA) journal indexes that do not have inclusion criteria, do not support interoperability of online searches, and contain exclusively predatory journals. This chapter presents some examples to illustrate how predators imitate the ecosystem of legitimate scholarly publishing in support of the predatory market.

8.1 Background

WoS's Journal impact factor (JIF) is calculated by using this formula:

$$\text{IF of a journal in year } X = \frac{\text{Citations in X to articles published in X}-1 \text{ and X}-2}{\text{Articles published in X}-1 \text{ and X}-2}$$

So, to get the JIF score of *PLOS One* in 2019, the calculation is as follows:

1. The total citations in 2019 of articles published in the journal in 2018 is 37,072.
2. The total citations in 2019 of articles published in the journal in 2017 is 67,793.
3. The total number of citable articles in the journal in 2018 is 17,878.
4. The total number of citable articles in the journal in 2017 is 20,393.
5. JIF = (37,072 + 67,793)/(17,878 + 20,393) = 104,865 / 38,271 = 2.740.

Below are the comparisons to the JIF values of some selected journals in the same year:

1. *New England Journal of Medicine* = 74.699
2. *Nature* = 42.779
3. *British Medical Journal* = 30.313
4. *Learned Publishing* = 2.606
5. *Serials Review* = 0.425

DOI: 10.4324/9781003029335-8

JIF is calculated for every journal indexed in WoS's multiple databases as a proxy for the relative importance of the journal within its academic discipline. Journals with higher JIF scores are considered more valuable, and present more intrinsic prestige in their respective subjects than journals with lower scores. The JIF data is maintained and provided by the Institute for Scientific Information (ISI), which later became part of Thomson Reuters and then of Clarivate Analytics, through the web platform WoS. Although the system has faced some criticism (Casadevall & Fang, 2014; Seglen, 1997; van Leeuwen, 2012; van Wesel, 2016), JIF has been extensively accepted as the standard of academic assessment across countries, influencing decisions on where to publish, whom to hire or promote, and how to award grants. Although it is not the only quantitative measure of academic journals, because journal-level metrics by WoS also include 5-Year Impact Factor, EigenFactor, Immediacy Index, Cited Half-Life, etc., JIF is unarguably the most popular one.

Inspired by JIF, Elsevier created its CiteScore (Van Noorden, 2016), measuring all journals in the Scopus database, which almost double the size of the WoS collections. It calculates citations of articles in the proceeding four years instead of two years, which is viewed as an improvement over JIF. Another advantage of CiteScore is its free accessibility, as opposed to the fee-based WoS.

WoS applies restrictive inclusion criteria and limits the number of new journals each year (Archambault & Larivière, 2009). Many OA journals are too young to establish their scholarly prestige, and therefore are not candidates for a JIF by WoS (McVeigh, 2004). In 2016, WoS provided its JIF scores for 1,040 OA journals, roughly 10% of all its rated journals. Although Elsevier collects more journals, its CiteScore is also provided for about the same proportion of its journals (Erfanmanesh, 2017). The majority of OA journals have been ignored for bibliometric measures by the recognized services, let alone predatory journals.

It is the responsibility of bibliometricians to formulate, analyze, and apply the convoluted metrics from WoS, Scopus, and others. The rest of the scholarly community does not have the knowledge, time, and interest to understand the complexity of all quantitative methods, and is inclined to accept the simplest version of the metrics, which is JIF. As a matter of fact, most individuals may not even be able to tell what an impact factor really is, how to calculate the score, or who designs it. JIF may only be an ambiguous concept to them.

8.2 Artificial metrics

Predators have quickly taken advantage of researchers' extensive recognition of JIF and their unfamiliarity with the impact factor. Artificial metrics were invented as soon as predatory journals started their business to resemble JIF in order to give the journals a feeling of legitimacy (Dadkhah *et al.*, 2016; Lukić *et al.*, 2014). It is found that many artificial metrics providers are hijackers who stole the identity of legitimate journals such as *Afinidad* and *Wulfenia*, as described in Chapter 6 (Jalalian, 2015). With the introduction of artificial metrics, these hijackers start stealing the reputation of WoS to mislead readers and authors.

Basically, they create a website and claim to provide impact factor scores for journals subscribed to their service. Many adopt a name that is very similar to JIF: for example, the Universal Impact Factor (UIF), the Global Impact Factor (GIF), and the International Journal Impact Factor (I-JIF). They set a fee scheme on the website in the form of service charges or membership dues. The typical customer is a predatory journal that is completely aware of the practice of the artificial metrics, but willingly pays for its service in exchange for a fake impact factor score. This journal will post the score at the most visible location on its own website. Such a score is usually between 2.000 and 20.000; not so low as to appear unappealing, but also not so high as to make it suspicious. A study found more than half of predatory journals mention such an artificial score (Shamseer *et al.*, 2017).

8.2.1 Scale of artificial metrics

In 2013, Jalalian and Mahboobi (2013) detected several bogus metrics including GIF, UIF, and JIF by the Global Institute for Scientific Information. Jalalian (2015) added more names to the list later; and Jeffrey Beall maintained another list, what he called "misleading metrics", on his scholarlyoa.org. At the same time, Gutierrez *et al.* (2015) made a list of 21 artificial metrics. In a more recent study, Xia and Smith (2018) collected 57 artificial metrics. In order to analyze the properties of the artificial metrics, they removed those that are no longer in business or that do not post any evaluation criteria and examined 36 metrics that have questionable practices (Table 8.1).

Most artificial metrics provide impact factor service for a considerable number of journals. As early as 2014, CiteFactor was found to have released its scores for 8,281 journal (Jalalian, 2015); the number increased to 12,178 in 2015. However, these numbers may not be verified, since many metrics also index journals and provide more journals in their indexes than what they actually provide a score for. A study that did verify impact factor services found that by 2017, IIFS (see Table 8.1 for abbreviations) calculated impact factor values for 158 journals, but indexed 1,317 journals, R-JIF computed scores for 70 titles out of its 186 indexed titles, and S-JIF provided scores for 650 journals but indexed 2,914 journals (Xia & Smith, 2018).

Table 8.1 Examples of artificial metrics

Provider	Abbrev.	URL	Status*
AE Global Index	AEIF	http://aeglobalindex.com/	Inactive
African Quality Centre for Journals	AQCJ	http://aqcj.org/index.html	Active
American Standards for Journals and Research	ASJR	www.journal-metrics.com/index.php	Active
CiteFactor	CiteFactor	www.citefactor.org/	Active
Cosmos Impact Factor	Cosmos	http://cosmosimpactfactor.com/	Active
Digital Identification Database System	DIDS	http://dids.info/	Inactive
Digital Online Identifier-Database System	DOI-JIF	http://doi-ds.org/doijif/	Active
Int'l Directory of Indexing and Impact Factor	DIIF	www.idiif.com/index.php	Active
Eurasian Scientific Journal Index	ESJI	http://esjindex.org/index.php	Active
General Impact Factor	GIF	http://generalif.com/index2.php	Active
Global Impact Factor	GIF	http://globalimpactfactor.com/	Active
Global Institute for Scientific Information	GISI-JIF	www.jifactor.com/	Active
Impact Factor Services for International Journals	IFSIJ	http://ifsij.com	Active
IndexCopernicus	ICI	journals.indexcopernicus.com	Active
Infobase Index	IBI	www.infobaseindex.com/	Active
International Accreditation and Research Council	IARC	www.iarcif.org	Active
International Impact Factor Services	IIFS	http://impactfactorservice.com/	Active
International Innovative Journal Impact Factor	II-JIF	https://iijif.com/indexing/	Inactive
International Institute of Organized Research	I2OR	www.i2or.com	Active
International Journal Impact Factor	I-JIF	internationaljournalimpactfactor.com	Active
International Scientific Indexing	ISI 1	http://isindexing.com/isi/	Active
International Scientific Institute	ISI 2	www.scijournal.org	Active
International Society for Research Activity	ISRA JIF	www.israjif.org/index.html	Active

Provider	Abbrev.	URL	Status*
Jour Informatics	JIR	www.iaset.us/	Active
Journals Impact Factor	JIFactor	http://jifactor.org	Active
Journal's International Compliance Index	JIC Index	https://jicindex.com	Active
Open Academic Journals Index	OAJI	http://oaji.net	Active
Prerna Society of Technical Ed and Research	PRERNA	www.prernasociety.org	Active
Research Journal Impact Factor	R-JIF	www.rjifactor.com	Active
Root Indexing	RI	www.rootindexing.com/	Active
Scholar Article Journal Index	SAJI	www.scholarimpact.org/	Active
Science Impact Factor	SIF	http://scienceimpactfactor.com	Active
Scientific Indexing Services	SIS	www.sindexs.org/	Inactive
Scientific Journal Impact Factor	S-JIF	http://sjifactor.com/	Active
Systematic Impact Factor	SIF	http://sifactor.org	Active
Universal Impact Factor	UIF	http://uifactor.blogspot.com	Active

(Source: Xia & Smith, 2018, Table 1)

* As of spring 2021

Of those that have revealed information about their business operations, most services are based in India, including those that post their locations as India on the websites, those that do not clearly state a location but are found in India through their domain registrations (Jalalian, 2015), and those that claim to operate in other countries but charge fees in Indian rupees (Xia & Smith, 2018). The cost for such a score varies, but mostly is lower than $200 USD annually. Many artificial metrics offer additional services, such as journal indexing, language editing, paper writing, and article-level metrics for a cost.

None of these alleged metrics providers responded to the studies cited.

8.2.2 Criteria to calculate artificial metrics

The service providers in Table 8.1 post their criteria for calculating impact factor scores on their websites. Such criteria may include one or all of the following: (i) citation analyses by adopting a formula resembling WoS's

110 *Metrics and indexes*

formula, (ii) non-citation measures, e.g., by evaluating scientific vigor, editorial quality, and publishing conditions of a journal, and (iii) an Article Published Score, i.e., the numerical value of a journal based on the total number of its annual articles.

Their proposed citation analyses do not look realistic. As discussed previously, articles in predatory journals rarely receive any citations, which are the indispensable data in any such impact factor calculations. Even for journals with cited articles, claimed citation analyses may not exist. This is confirmed by the study of Xia and Smith (2018) that tested the algorithms of some artificial metrics for selected journals. Using these providers' formulas to divide citations retrieved through Google Scholar and Microsoft Academic by the total numbers of articles, their study reveals a large discrepancy between the scores and what are reported on the websites. The impact factors provided by these services in Table 8.1 look artificial and random and are hardly reproducible.

The second method to calculate impact factor scores is similarly unreliable. Although the metrics providers have varied criteria for a non-citation analysis, they all focus on qualitative measures of articles, journals, reviews, editorial work, and publishing process. The measures are unquantifiable and depend on an individual's judgment. With subjective opinions being converted into numerical values, the scoring mechanism can hardly be usable to rank publications, especially for the computation of impact factor values.

The inclusion of the Article Publication Scores in journal scoring is an invention of several artificial metrics such as GIF, R-JIF, and II-JIF. It is as simple as assigning numerical values to a journal based on the number of its annual publications. Hence, if a journal has published 451–500 articles in a given year, for example, it will receive an impact factor score of 1.000; if it

Table 8.2 Examples of alternative indexes

Alternative index	Abbrev.	# Journals
Publication Impact Factor	PIF	6,106
Cosmos	Cosmos	3,750
Directory of Research Journals Indexing	DRJI	3,497
Global Impact Factor	GIF	3,329
International Scientific Indexing	ISI	3,307
International Society for Research Activity	ISRA	1,412
International Impact Factor Services	IIFS	1,317
Global Science Citation Impact Factor	GS-CIF	1,137
Science Impact Factor	SIF	285
Scholar Article Impact Factor	SAIF	133

(Source: Xia 2019, Table 3)

has only published 0–55 articles, its score will be 0.555 (see Xia & Smith, 2018, Table 6). This scoring system favors mega-journals that have been increasingly popular in OA journal publishing (Shen & Björk, 2015). However, it is by no means a scientific measure of a journal's scholarly prestige, and has nothing in common with JIF scores.

8.3 Alternative indexes

Both WoS and Scopus index high-quality, peer-reviewed research journals and provide usage data of, and citation analysis for, these journals. Other legitimate services may only offer indexation, such as Medline and PsycInfo. the Directory of Open Access Journals (DOAJ) is a known index for OA journals. Because all recognized indexing services adopt a restrictive journal inclusion policy to select only those that can meet their criteria of high scholarly and publishing quality, predatory journals have been largely excluded. This presents a good opportunity for the predatory market to serve OA journals that cannot become candidates for DOAJ or other indexes.

There is no source revealing how many indexing services for predatory journals are active, partially because it is an unstable business. Many disappear quickly and are replaced by new providers. Some of the alternative indexes that are still in business are operated by the same providers listed in Table 8.1 that produce artificial metrics. In other words, many fake impact factor providers also index OA journals. Xia (2019) analyzed a total of 21 indexing services. The services in Table 8.2 are part of his analysis that include the total number of their indexed journals. It shows that they have a varied number of journals. The largest index collects over 6,000 journals, while the smallest only indexes just over 100. Except for one index, all others also provide journal metrics alongside journal indexing. For the combined services, each provider maintains a longer list of indexed journals than the list of journals that are provided an impact factor score. This is because their services for score calculations are mostly fee-based, while indexation is typically free of charge. For a journal to be indexed, it only needs to submit its title, the International Standard Serial Number (ISSN), country, publisher, frequency, and other basic publishing data, without needing to provide any evidence related to quality control, such as evidence of peer review activities.

The alternative service providers and the indexed predatory journals mutually benefit from the business. On the one hand, the providers increase potential subscribers to their fee-based service, namely, the calculation of impact factor scores, by indexing journals in their databases and providing access to the public. On the other hand, the journals being indexed increase their visibility by appearing in as many journal indexes as possible, even if some are questionable in practice and quality. Some non-predatory journals, including subscription-based journals and legitimate OA journals, are found to cite artificial metrics (Shamseer *et al.*, 2017). This helps explain Jalalian's observation that the exposure of a journal seems to outweigh its academic reputation:

> In one specific case, I called the Editor-in-Chief of a high-quality, university-based medical journal to ask him to remove the metrics assigned to his journal by one of the most "reputable" fake impact factor companies. Much to my amazement and disappointment, he refused to do so even though he knew that the metric was fake.
> (Jalalian, 2015, p. 1071)

However, the majority of the journals indexed by the alternative services are predatory journals. Xia (2019) compared journal titles in the indexes listed in Table 8.2 to journals in Beall's journal blacklist, as well as to the DOAJ whitelist, and found a high rate of overlap between individual alternative indexes and the blacklist, and among the alternative indexes. In contrast, the rate of overlap between individual alternative indexes and the whitelist is relatively low.

The websites of the alternative indexing services are not designed with interoperability in mind. Readers will need to search each individual website to find its included journals, rather than being able to search them through Google or other search engines. Lack of knowledge of web technology may be the reason, but the designers may also be intentionally hiding their activities because they only care about how to make a profit, but understand that their business is deceptive in nature.

8.4 Conclusion

Artificial metrics are unreproducible. They are not alternatives to JIF, but are designed to make a profit and serve predatory publications. It has become apparent that artificial metrics and predatory journals are interdependent. The former creates artificial scores for the latter in exchange for money, while the latter purchases the scores, although they may not actually trust them, to make themselves attractive to readers and authors.

The same providers offering artificial impact factors also index OA journals, but the latter service is typically free of charge. The providers have an interest in expanding their list of journals to promote business and attract more subscribers to their service of fake impact factor scores. They attempt to imitate the infrastructure of legitimate metrics and indexation, such as WoS, but have to rely on cheating behaviors because they basically serve predatory publications.

9 Conclusion

This book has exposed various practices of predatory publishing and the impacts they have created on science, scholarly infrastructure, decision-making, people's perspectives and attitudes, and our lives. The immediate threat of predatory publishing to scholarship dissemination, mainly on publications, conferences, and bibliometrics, has received increasing recognition by the scholarly community over the past decades. However, very few are fully acquainted with the multifaceted aspects of the business; the majority of people cannot tell how to distinguish predatory behaviors from legitimate business, and are unaware of the consequences of getting involved in predatory publishing. To help more people understand this type of academic misconduct, this book has attempted to paint an overarching picture of predatory publishing.

It started by introducing the radical changes in scholarly communication that have shifted publications from print to online versions because of technological revolutions. It then focused on describing the switch in publishing from subscription-based access to open access, and how such a move has facilitated the development and expansion of fraudulent publishing. When authors, institutions, and funding agencies began to support free, immediate, and online sharing of information and data, the market of scholarly publishing adopted alternative ways of regaining commercial viability. However, this time, the rebalancing of the market has come at the cost of quality control.

Predatory publishing has benefited from the long-standing academic tradition of publish-or-perish, which, on the one hand, pushes researchers in their scientific pursuits, but on the other hand, creates tremendous pressure on individuals who have to contend with policies that favor the quantity of publications. This book argues that when the publish-or-perish model is introduced in many developing countries where technological infrastructure has not yet been fully developed, globalization efforts have forced

DOI: 10.4324/9781003029335-9

institutions and individuals there to face the change in local standards and compete with those in developed countries, even though such competition is unfair due to language barriers, different levels of training, and so on. Predatory publishers seize upon this unfairness and take the opportunity to exploit the new culture and gain a foothold.

Predators create scholarly journals and organize professional conferences to serve academics whose papers cannot meet the standards of academic publications, but whose careers need the support of publications. These predators design their products to give them a professional look by providing artificial metrics and promising quality controls that don't exist. They adopt deceptive strategies to cheat authors in return for article processing fees or conference registrations, while the authors cheat their institutions with their authorship in predatory journals or their services in predatory activities in exchange for career growth. Throughout the book, cheating behaviors by predators as well as by individual researchers were discussed. It expressed how authors were victimized in the early days, but have become knowing participants recently. It also described how governments in many developing countries have gotten increasingly involved in fighting predatory businesses by revising their academic policies and collaborating with institutions to adjust their assessment criteria.

This manuscript details popularly recognized criteria that identify predatory behaviors, as well as products developed by applying the criteria: namely, the blacklists of predatory publishers, journals, conferences, metrics, and indexes. The development of, and debate over, predatory watchdogs are extensively reviewed, especially Jeffrey Beall's controversial but well-received lists and their application in the verification of quality publishing outlets, coupled with the discussion of the journal whitelists by the Directory of Open Access Journals (DOAJ) and Cabells. Additionally, the book has introduced various types of less-noticed efforts, such as home-grown watchlists and safelists by professional associations, individual institutions, and government agencies, shedding light on an increasing awareness of, and safeguarding against, unethical and unprofessional publishing business by the scholarly community and beyond.

Predatory publishing is a complicated practice, which makes the identification of predatory journals difficult in some cases. Many predatory publishers constantly adjust their operations, and may have evolved their deceptive businesses with increasingly sophisticated systems. With the appearance of legitimacy, although only at face value, they have been able to attract a large number of submissions, whether unsuspecting or deliberate, to make their business successful in terms of revenue and size. This book reported selected cases to illustrate possible strategies adopted by questionable publishers, and points out scenarios wherein a publisher establishes

Conclusion 115

credibility through the content of some of its publications to acquire scholarly reputation, while maintaining its easy acceptance of low-quality submissions for the rest of its products for profit. It is the commercial greed of a publisher that drives its possible bipolar practices and makes the predatory market thriving but messy.

This book has also explored criminal activities detected in scholarly publishing. Criminals take advantage of web technologies to hijack legitimate journals by stealing their identities and intercepting their payment income. Such activities are rarely known to the scholarly community, but present more serious challenges to scholarly publishing. Similarly, a call for attention to the enthusiastic participation of major pharmaceutical companies in predatory conferences is also presented in this manuscript, as are the potential damages to medical practice of such participation.

Alongside the rapid expansion in the scale of predatory publishing, the literature to expose predatory behaviors has also surged in the form of scientific analysis, newspaper reports, online papers, social media discussion, etc. The past couple of years, in particular, have witnessed an exponential growth of publications on predatory publishing, mainly in the fields of biomedicine. This increase represents a growth of awareness among scholars and the public about academic misconduct. As stated in the introduction, the author only hopes that this book serves as one reference source from which readers will become familiar with the origins and evolution of predatory publishing, and will understand how to find other materials on this topic for further exploration.

Appendix A
Slightly modified Beall's third version of criteria for predatory behaviors

Editor and Staff
1. Publisher serves as journal editor
2. No single individual is identified as journal's editor
3. Journal does not identify a formal editorial/review board
4. Editor, or staff, or board members have no academic information such as institutional affiliation
5. Evidence shows that editor and/or review board members do not possess relevant academic expertise
6. Journal editorial board serves on other journals of the same publisher
7. Board members are fewer than two or three, listed without their knowledge or permission, or are ghost members
8. Board members have little or no geographical diversity, though journal claims an international scope or coverage
9. Editorial board engages in gender bias (i.e., exclusion of any female members)

Business Management
1. No transparency in publishing operations
2. No policies/practices for digital preservation, so if journal ceases operations, its content disappears from the internet
3. Publish a large fleet of journals, often using a common template to quickly create each journal's webpage

Integrity
1. Journal title is incongruent with its mission
2. Journal title does not adequately reflect its origin (e.g., "Canadian Journal . . ." does not have any Canada connection)
3. Journal falsely claims impact factor or an exaggerated international standing in spam emails or on its website
4. Publisher sends spam requests for peer reviews to scholars unqualified to review submissions
5. Publisher falsely claims legitimate indexing
6. No sufficient resources exist to prevent and eliminate author misconduct
7. Publisher asks corresponding author to suggest reviewers without adequately vetting their qualifications/authenticity

Other
1. Re-publish papers but do not provide appropriate credits
2. Use boastful language like "leading publisher" even though publisher may only be a startup or a novice organization
3. Use a Western country address but operate from a developing country

Business Management	Other
4 Provide insufficient or hide information about author fees	4 Provide minimal or no copyediting or proofreading
5 Do not allow search engines to crawl their content and prevent content from being indexed in academic indexes	5 Publish papers that are not academic at all, e.g., essays by laypeople, polemical editorials, or obvious pseudo-science
6 Copy-proof (lock) their PDFs, making it harder to check for plagiarism	6 Its "contact us" page only includes a web form or an email address, and publisher hides or does not reveal its location

(With permission from Jeffrey Beall)

Appendix B
Cabells's criteria for predatory practices, version 1.1

Category	Criterion	Level
Integrity	The same article appears in more than one journal	Severe
	Hijacked journal (defined as a fraudulent website created to look like a legitimate academic journal for the purpose of offering academics the opportunity to rapidly publish their research for a fee)	Severe
	Information received from the journal does not match the journal's website	Severe
	The journal or publisher claims to be a non-profit when it is actually a for profit company	Severe
	The owner/Editor of the journal or publisher falsely claims academic positions or qualifications	Severe
	The journal is associated with a conference that has been identified as predatory	Severe
	The journal gives a fake ISSN	Severe
	The title of the journal is copied or so similar to that of a legitimate journal that it could cause confusion between the two	Moderate
	The name of the journal references a country or demographic that does not relate to the content or origin of the journal	Moderate
	The journal uses language that suggests that it is industry leading, but is in fact a new journal	Moderate
	The journal/publisher hides or obscures relationships with for-profit partner companies that could result in corporate manipulation of science	Moderate

Cabells's criteria for predatory practices 119

Category	Criterion	Level
	Insufficient resources are spent on preventing and eliminating author misconduct that may result in repeated cases of plagiarism, self-plagiarism, image manipulation, etc. (no policies regarding plagiarism, ethics, misconduct, etc., no use of plagiarism screens)	Minor
	The journal/publisher hides or obscures information regarding associated publishing imprints or parent companies	Minor
Peer Review	No editor or editorial board listed on the journal's website at all	Severe
	Editors do not actually exist or are deceased	Severe
	The journal includes scholars on an editorial board without their knowledge or permission	Severe
	Evident data that little to no peer review is being done and the journal claims to be "peer reviewed"	Severe
	The journal has a large editorial board but very few articles are published per year	Moderate
	Inadequate peer review (i.e., a single reader reviews submissions; peer reviewers read papers outside their field of study; etc.)	Moderate
	The journal's website does not have a clearly stated peer review policy	Moderate
	The founder of the publishing company is the editor of all of the journals published by said company	Moderate
	Evident data showing that the editor/review board members do not possess academic expertise to reasonably qualify them to be publication gatekeepers in the journal's field	Moderate
	No affiliations are given for editorial board members and/or editors	Moderate
	Little geographical diversity of board members and the journal claims to be International	Moderate
	The journal includes board members who are prominent researchers but exempt them from any contribution to the journal except the use of their names and/or photographs	Moderate
	Editorial board members (appointed over 2 years ago) have not heard from the journal at all since being appointed to the board	Moderate

(Continued)

Cabells's criteria for predatory practices

Category	Criterion	Level
Publication Practices	The journal publishes papers that are not academic at all, e.g., essays by laypeople or obvious pseudo-science	Severe
	No articles are published or the archives are missing issues and/or articles	Severe
	Falsely claims indexing in well-known databases (especially SCOPUS, DOAJ, JCR, and Cabells)	Severe
	Falsely claims universities or other organizations as partners or sponsors	Severe
	Machine-generated or other "sting" abstracts or papers are accepted	Severe
	No copyediting	Moderate
	Little geographical diversity of authors and the journal claims to be International	Moderate
	The Editor publishes research in his own journal	Moderate
	The journal purposefully publishes controversial articles in the interest of boosting citation count	Moderate
	The journal publishes papers presented at conferences without additional peer review	Moderate
	The name of the publisher suggests that it is a society, academy, etc. when it is only a publisher and offers no real benefits to members	Moderate
	The name of the publisher suggests that it is a society, academy, etc. when it is only a solitary proprietary operation and does not meet the definition of the term used or implied non-profit mission	Moderate
	Authors are published several times in the same journal and/or issue	Moderate
	Similarly titled articles published by same author in more than one journal	Moderate
	The publisher displays prominent statements that promise rapid publication and/or unusually quick peer review (less than 4 weeks)	Moderate
	The number of articles published has increased by 75% or more in the last year	Moderate
	The number of articles published has increased by 50–74% in the last year	Moderate
	The number of articles published has increased by 25–49% in the last year	Minor

Cabells's criteria for predatory practices 121

Category	Criterion	Level
Indexing & Metrics	The journal uses misleading metrics (i.e., metrics with the words "impact factor" that are not the Clarivate Analytics Impact Factor)	Severe
	The publisher or its journals are not listed in standard periodical directories or are not widely catalogued in library databases	Minor
Fees	The journal offers options for researchers to prepay APCs for future articles	Severe
	The journal states there is an APC or another fee but does not give information on the amount or gives conflicting information	Severe
	The journal or publisher offers membership to receive discounts on APCs but does not give information on how to become a member and/or on the membership fees	Severe
	The author must pay APC or publication fee before submitting the article (specifically calls the fee a publication fee, not a submission fee)	Severe
	The journal does not indicate that there are any fees associated with publication, review, submission, etc. but the author is charged a fee after submitting a manuscript	Severe
	The publisher or journal's website seems too focused on the payment of fees	Moderate
Access & Copyright	States the journal is completely open access but not all articles are openly available	Moderate
	No way to access articles (no information on open access or how to subscribe)	Moderate
	The journal is open access but no information is given about how the journal is supported financially (i.e., author fees, advertising, sponsorship, etc.)	Moderate
	No policies for digital preservation	Moderate
	The journal has a poorly written copyright policy and/or transfer form that does not actually transfer copyright	Moderate
	The journal publishes not in accordance with their copyright or does not operate under a copyright license	Moderate
Business Practices	The journal has been asked to quit sending emails and has not stopped	Moderate
	The journal or publisher gives a business address in a Western country but the majority of authors are based in developing countries	Moderate

(*Continued*)

Category	Criterion	Level
	Emailed solicitations for manuscripts from the journal are received by researchers who are clearly not in the field the journal covers	Moderate
	Email invitations for editorial board members or reviewers from the journal are received by researchers who are clearly not in the field the journal covers	Moderate
	Multiple emails received from a journal in a short amount of time	Moderate
	Emails received from a journal do not include the option to unsubscribe to future emails	Moderate
	The journal copy proofs and locks PDFs	Moderate
	No subscribers/nobody uses the journal	Minor
	The journal's website does not allow web crawlers	Minor

(Source: Toutloff, 2019. With permission from Cabells International)

References

1 Introduction

Anderson, R. (2015). Should we retire the term "predatory publishing"? *The Scholarly Kitchen*, 11 May. https://scholarlykitchen.sspnet.org/2015/05/11/should-we-retire-the-term-predatory-publishing/.

Anderson, R. (2019). *OSI issue brief 3: Deceptive publishing*. Open Scholarship Initiative. doi:10.13021/osi2019.241.

Beall, J. (2009). Bentham open. *The Charleston Advisor* 11(1): 29–32.

Beall, J. (2012). *Criteria for determining predatory open-access publishers*, 2nd edition. https://scholarlyoa.files.wordpress.com/2012/11/criteria-2012-2.pdf.

Beall, J. (2013). Predatory publishing is just one of the consequences of gold open access. *Learned Publishing* 26(2): 79–84. doi:10.1087/20130203.

Beall, J. (2015). *Criteria for determining predatory open-access publishers*, 3rd edition. https://beallslist.weebly.com/uploads/3/0/9/5/30958339/criteria-2015.pdf.

Björk, B.C., Kanto-Karvonen, S., & Harviainen, J.T. (2020). How frequently are articles in predatory open access journals cited. *Publications* 8(17). doi:10.3390/publications8020017.

Cobey, K.D., Lalu, M.M., Skidmore, B., et al. (2018). What is a predatory journal? A scoping review. *F1000Research*. doi:10.12688/f1000resaerch.15256.2.

Cukier, S., Lalu, M., Bryson, G.L., et al. (2020). Defining predatory journals and responding to the threat they pose: A modified Delphi consensus process. *BMJ Open* 10(2). doi:10.1136/bmjopen-2019-035561.

Eriksson, S., & Helgesson, G. (2017). The false academy: Predatory publishing in science and bioethics. *Medicine, Health Care and Philosophy* 20(2): 163–170. doi:10.1007/s11019-016-9740-3.

Eysenbach, G. (2008). Black sheep among open access journals and publishers. *Random Research Rants*, March. http://gunther-eysenbach.blogspot.com/2008/03/black-sheep-among-open-access-journals.html.

Grudniewicz, A., Moher, D., Cobey, K.D., et al. (2019). Predatory journals: No definition, no defense. *Nature* 576: 210–212. doi:10.1038/d41586-019-03759-y.

Kendall, G. (2021). Beall's legacy in the battle against predatory publishers. *Learned Publishing*, Early view. doi:10.1002/leap.1374.

Mertkan, S., Aliusta, G.O., & Suphi, N. (2021). Knowledge production on predatory publishing: A systematic review. *Learned Publishing* Early view. doi:10.1002/leap.1380.

Moher, D., Shamseer, L., Cobey, K.D., *et al.* (2017). Stop this waste of people, animals and money. *Nature* 549: 23–25. doi:10.1038/549023a.

Molchanova, A., Chunikhina, N., & Strielkowski, W. (2017). Innovations and academic publishing: Who will cast the first stone? *Marketing and Management of Innovations* 4: 40–48. doi:10.21272/mmi.2017.4-03.

Olivarez, J.D., Bales, S., Sare, L., *et al.* (2018). Format aside: Applying Beall's criteria to assess the predatory nature of both OA and non-OA library and information science journals. *College & Research Libraries* 79(1). doi:10.5860/crl.79.1.52.

Perlin, M.S., Imasato, T., & Borensein, D. (2018). Is predatory publishing a real threat? Evidence from a large database study. *Scientometrics* 116(1): 255–273. doi:10.1007/s11192-018-2750-6.

Poynder, R. (2008). The open access interviews: Dove medical press. *Open and Shut?* 5 November. https://poynder.blogspot.com/2008/11/open-access-interviews-dove-medical.html.

Shen, C., & Björk, B.C. (2015). "Predatory" open access: A longitudinal study of article volumes and market characteristics. *BMC Medicine* 13(1): 230. doi:10.1186/s12916-015-0469-2.

Strinzel, M., Severin, A., Milzow, K., *et al.* (2019). "Blacklists" and "whitelists" to tackle predatory publishing: A cross-sectional comparison and thematic analysis. *mBio* 10: e00411–e00441.

Teixeira da Silva, J.A. (2017). Caution with the continued use of Jeffrey Beall's "predatory" open access publishing lists. *AME Medical Journal* 2: 97. doi:10.21037/amj.2017.06.14.

Umlauf, M.G., & Mochizuki, Y. (2018). Predatory publishing and cybercrime targeting academics. *International Journal of Nursing Practice* 24(S1). doi:10.1111/ijn.12656.

2 Background

Abritis, A., & McCook, A. (2017). Cash bonuses for peer-reviewed papers go global. *Science* 357(6351): 541. doi:10.1126/science.357.6351.541.

Adomi, E.E., & Mordi, C. (2003). Publication in foreign journals and promotion of academics in Nigeria. *Learned Publishing* 16(4): 259–263.

Armstrong, M. (2014). *Open access to research*. MPRA Paper #59731. https://mpra.ub.uni-muenchen.de/59731/.

Berger, M. (2017). Everything you ever wanted to know about predatory publishing but were afraid to ask. *The Conference of ACRL 2017*, 22–25 March, Baltimore, MD. https://academicworks.cuny.edu/ny_pubs/141/.

Biagioli, M. (2002). From book censorship to academic peer review. *Emergences* 12(1): 11–45.

Björk, B.C., Welling, P., Laakso, M., *et al.* (2010). Open access to the scientific journal literature: Situation 2009. *PLoS One* 5(6): e11273. doi:10.1371/journal.pone.0011273.

References

Bohannon, J. (2013). Who's afraid of peer review? *Science* 342(6154): 60–65. doi:10.1126/science.342.6154.60.

Branin, J.J., & Case, M. (1998). Reforming scholarly publishing in the sciences: A librarian perspective. *Notes of the AMS* 45(4): 475–486.

Brown, M.J.I. (2015). Vanity and predatory academic publishers are corrupting the pursuit of knowledge. *The Conversation*, 2 August. https://theconversation.com/vanity-and-predatory-academic-publishers-are-corrupting-the-pursuit-of-knowledge-45490.

Budzinski, O., Grebel, T., Wolling, J., *et al.* (2020). Drivers of article processing charges in open access. *Scientometrics* 124: 2185–2206. doi:10.1007/s11192-020-03578-3.

Crawford, W. (2017). Gray OA 2012–2016: Open access journals beyond DOAJ. *Cites & Insights* 17(1): 1–68. http://citesandinsights.info/civ17i1.pdf.

Davis, P. (2009). Open access publisher accepts nonsense manuscript for dollars. *Scholarly Kitchen*, 10 June. https://scholarlykitchen.sspnet.org/2009/06/10/nonsense-for-dollars/.

Denisova-Schmidt, E. (2020). *Corruption in higher education: Global challenges and responses*. Leiden: Brill Publishers.

de Rond, M., & Miller, A.N. (2005). Publish or perish: Bane or boon of academic life. *Journal of Management Inquiry* 14(4): 321–329. doi:10.1177/1056492605276850.

Dyrud, M.A. (2014). Predatory online technical journals: A question of ethics. *The 121st ASEE Annual Conference & Exposition*, 15–18 June, Indianapolis, IN. Paper ID #8413.

Garanayak, S., & Ramaiah, C.K. (2019). Predatory journals publishing trend in India: A study. *University News* 57(38): 11–18.

Hedding, D.W. (2019). Payouts push professors towards predatory journals. *Nature* 565: 267. doi:10.1038/d41586-019-00120-1.

Hirst, P., Thompson, G., & Bromley, S. (2009). *Globalization in question*. London: Polity Press.

Houghton, J.W. (2010). Economic implications of alternative publishing models: Self-archiving and repositories. *LIBER Quarterly* 19(3–4): 275–292. doi:10.18352/lq.7966.

Kelly, J., Sadeghieh,T., & Adeli, K. (2014). Peer review in scientific publications: Benefits, critiques, & a survival guide. *The Journal of the International Federation of Clinical Chemistry and Laboratory Medicine* 25(3). www.ncbi.nlm.nih.gov/pmc/articles/PMC4975196/.

Kozok, U. (2017). *Predatory publishing: A case story*. https://ipll.manoa.hawaii.edu/internal/documents/predatory-publishers/.

Krawczyk, F., & Kulczyki, E. (2021). How is open access accused of being predatory? The impact of Beall's lists of predatory journals on academic publishing. *Journal of Academic Librarianship* 47(2). doi:10.1016/j.acalib.2020.102271.

Kutz, M. (2002). The scholars rebellion against scholarly publishing practices: Varmus, Vitek, and Venting. *Searcher* 10(1). www.infotoday.com/searcher/jan02/kutz.htm.

Laakso, M., Welling, P., Bukvova, H., *et al.* (2011). The development of open access journal publishing from 1993 to 2009. *PLoS One* 6(6): e20961. doi:10.1371/journal.pone.0020961.

References

Laquintano, T. (2013). The legacy of the vanity press and digital transitions. *The Journal of Electronic Publishing* 16(1). doi:10.3998/3336451.0016.104.

Miller, A.N., Taylor, S.G., & Bedeian, A.G. (2010). Publish or perish: Academic life as management faculty live it. *Career Development International* 16(5): 422–445. doi:10.1108/13620431111167751.

Nwagwu, W.E. (2016). Open access in the developing regions: Situating the altercations about predatory publishing. *Canadian Journal of Information and Library Science* 40(1): 58–80.

Olijhoek, T., Mitchell, D., & Bjørnshauge, L. (2015). Criteria for open access and publishing. *ScienceOpen Research*. doi:10.14293/S2199-1006.1.SOR-EDU.AMHUHV.v1.

Omobowale, A.O., Akanle, O., Adeniran, A.I., et al. (2014). Peripheral scholarship and the context of foreign paid publishing in Nigeria. *Current Sociology* 62(5): 666–684. doi:10.1177/0011392113508127.

Putnam, G.H. (1897). *Authors and publishers: A manual of suggestions for beginners in literature*. New York: G.P. Putnam's Sons.

Qiu, J. (2010). Publish or perish in China. *Nature* 463: 142–143. doi:10.1038/463142a.

Quan, W., Chen, B., & Shu, F. (2017). Publish or improverish: An investigation of the monetary reward system of science in China (1999–2016). *Aslib Journal of Information Management* 69(5): 486–502. doi:10.1108/AJIM-01-2017-0014.

Quint, B. (2002). BioMed Central begins charging authors and their institutions for article publishing. *Information Today*, 7 January. http://newsbreaks.infotoday.com/nbreader.asp?ArticleID=17276.

Sample, I. (2014). How computer-generated fake papers are flooding academia. *The Guardian*. www.theguardian.com/technology/shortcuts/2014/feb/26/how-computer-generated-fake-papers-flooding-academia/.

Solomon, D., & Björk, B.C. (2012). A study of open access journals using article processing charges. *JASIS&T: Journal of the Association for Information Science and Technology* 63(8): 1485–1495. doi:10.1002/asi.22673.

Spier, R. (2002). The history of the peer-review process. *Trends in Biotechnology* 20(8): 357–358. doi:10.1016/S0167-7799(02)01985-6.

SQW. (2004). *Costs and business models in scientific research publishing*. London: The Wellcome Trust. https://wellcome.org/sites/default/files/wtd003184_0.pdf.

Stromberg, J. (2014). I sold my undergraduate thesis to a print content farm. *The Slate*, 23 March. https://slate.com/technology/2014/03/lap-lambert-academic-publishing-my-trip-to-a-print-content-farm.html.

Suber, P. (2015). *Open access overview*. https://legacy.earlham.edu/~peters/fos/overview.htm/.

Sullivan, H.A. (1958). Vanity press publishing. *Library Trends* 7(1): 105–115.

Tomlinson, J. (1999). *Globalization and culture*. Chicago, IL: The University of Chicago Press.

van Dalen, H.P., & Henkens, K. (2012). Intended and unintended consequences of a publish-or-perish culture: A worldwide survey. *JASIS&T: Journal of the Association for Information Science and Technology* 63(7): 1282–1293. doi:10.1002/asi.22636.

Wallace, F.H., & Perri, T.J. (2018). Economists behaving badly: Publications in predatory journals. *Scientometrics* 115: 749–766. doi:10.1007/s11192-018-2690-1.
Xia, J. (2019). Economic modelling of predatory journal publishing. *Publishing Research Quarterly* 35(3): 377–390. doi:10.1007/s12109-019-09661-9.
Xia, J., Harmon, J.L., Connolly, K.G., et al. (2015). Who publishes in "predatory" journals? *JASIS&T: Journal of the Association for Information Science and Technology* 66(7): 1406–1417. doi:10.1002/asi.23265.

3 Journals

ABDC. (2019). *2019 journal quality list review final report.* Kensington, Australia: Australian Business Deans Council, 6 December. https://abdc.edu.au/wp-content/uploads/2020/03/abdc-2019-journal-quality-list-review-report-6-december-2019_2.pdf.
Anderson, R. (2017). Cabell's new predatory journal blacklist: A review. *The Scholarly Kitchen*, 25 July. https://scholarlykitchen.sspnet.org/2017/07/25/cabells-new-predatory-journal-blacklist-review/.
Anderson, R. (2019a). Cabell's new predatory journal blacklist: An updated review. *The Scholarly Kitchen*, 1 May. https://scholarlykitchen.sspnet.org/2019/05/01/cabells-predatory-journal-blacklist-an-updated-review/.
Anderson, R. (2019b). Citation contamination: References to predatory journals in the legitimate scientific literature. *The Scholarly Kitchen*, 28 October. https://scholarlykitchen.sspnet.org/2019/10/28/citation-contamination-references-to-predatory-journals-in-the-legitimate-scientific-literature/.
Bagues, M., Sylos-Labinib, M., & Zinovyeva, N. (2019). A walk on the wild side: "Predatory" journals and information asymmetries in scientific evaluations. *Research Policy* 48: 462–477. doi:10.1016/j.respol.2018.04.013.
Beall, J. (2012). Predatory publishers and opportunities for scholarly societies. *The American Educational Research Association Meeting*, Washington, DC, 8–10 November. http://eprints.rclis.org/18044/.
Beall, J. (2013). Predatory publishing is just one of the consequences of gold open access. *Learned Publishing* 26(2): 79–84. doi:10.1087/20130203.
Beall, J. (2017). What I learned from predatory publishers. *Biochemia Medica* 27(2): 273–278. doi:10.11613/BM.2017.029.
Berger, M., & Cirasella, J. (2015). Beyond Beall's list. *College & Research Libraries News* 76(3): 132–135. https://crln.acrl.org/index.php/crlnews/article/view/9277/10342.
Bisaccio, M. (2018). Cabells' journal whitelist and blacklist: Intelligent data for informed journal evaluations. *Learned Publishing* 31(3): 243–248. doi:10.1002/leap.1164.
Björk, B.C., Kanto-Karvonen, S., & Harviainen, J.T. (2020). How frequently are articles in predatory open access journals cited. *Publications* 8(17). doi:10.3390/publications8020017.
Björk, B.C., & Solomon, D. (2014). *Developing an effective market for open access article processing charges.* London: Wellcome Trust.

Blobaum, P. (2018). Cabells scholarly analytics: A go-to source on journal quality (Review). *Faculty Research and Creative Activity* 35. https://opus.govst.edu/faculty/35.

Bohannon, J. (2013). Who's afraid of peer review? *Science* 342(6154): 60–65. doi:10.1126/science.342.6154.60.

Chen, X. (2019). Beall's list and Cabell's blacklist: A comparison of two lists of predatory OA journals. *Serials Review* 45(4): 219–226. doi:10.1080/00987913.2019.1694810.

Clemons, M., Silva, M., Joy, A.A., et al. (2017). Predatory invitations from journals: More than just a nuisance? *The Oncologist* 22: 236–240. doi:10.1634/theoncologist.2016-0371.

Cobey, K.D., Grudniewicz, A., Lalu, M.M., et al. (2019). Knowledge and motivations of researchers publishing in presumed predatory journals: A survey. *BMJ Open* 9(3): e026516. doi:10.1136/bmjopen-2018-026516.

Cobey, K.D., Lalu, M.M., Skidmore, B., et al. (2018). What is a predatory journal? A scoping review. *F1000Research*. doi:10.12688/f1000resaerch.15256.2.

Colvin, J.B., & Vinyard, M. (2016). Cabell's international. *The Charleston Advisor* 18(1): 9–14. doi:10.5260/chara.18.1.9.

Crawford, W. (2014). Ethics and access 1: The sad case of Jeffrey Beall. *Cites & Insights* 14(4): 1–14. https://citesandinsights.info/civ14i4.pdf/.

Crawford, W. (2017a). Gray OA 2012–2016: Open access journals beyond DOAJ. *Cites & Insights* 17(1): 1–68. http://citesandinsights.info/civ17i1.pdf.

Crawford, W. (2017b). Gray OA 2014–2017: A partial follow-up. *Cites & Insights* 17(9): 1–38. https://citesandinsights.info/civ17i9.pdf.

Cyranoski, D. (2018). China awaits controversial blacklist of "poor quality" journals. *Nature* 562: 471–472. doi:10.1038/d41586-018-07025-5.

Dony, C., Raskinet, M., Renaville, F., et al. (2020). How reliable and useful is Cabell's blacklist: A data-driven analysis. *LIBER Quarterly* 30: 1–38. doi:10.18352/lq.10339.

Eriksson, S., & Helgesson, G. (2017). The false academy: Predatory publishing in science and bioethics. *Medicine, Health Care and Philosophy* 20(2): 163–170. doi:10.1007/s11019-016-9740-3.

Forrester, A., Björk, B.C., & Tenopir, C. (2017). New web services that help authors choose journals. *Learned Publishing* 30(4): 281–287. doi:10.1002/leap.1112.

Hedlund, T., & Rabow, I. (2009). Scholarly publishing and open access in the Nordic countries. *Learned Publishing* 22(3): 177–186. doi:10.1087/2009303.

Kendall, G. (2021). Beall's legacy in the battle against predatory publishers. *Learned Publishing*, Early view. doi:10.1002/leap.1374.

Kurt, S. (2018). Why do authors publish in predatory journals. *Learned Publishing* 31: 141–147. doi:10.1002/leap.1150.

Linacre, S. (2019). The journal blacklist surpasses the 12,000 journals listed mark. *The Source*, 2 October. https://blog.cabells.com/2019/10/02/the-journal-blacklist-surpasses-the-12000-journals-listed-mark/.

Linacre, S. (2020). Growth of predatory publishing shows no sign of slowing. *The Source*, 26 February. https://blog.cabells.com/2020/02/26/growth-of-predatory-publishing-shows-no-sign-of-slowing/.

Marchitelli, A., Galimberti, P., Bollini, A., et al. (2017). Improvement of editorial quality of journals indexed in DOAJ: A data analysis. *JLIS.it* 8(1): 1–21. doi:10.4403/jlis.it-12052.

Markowitz, D., Powell, J., & Hancock, J. (2014). The writing style of predatory publishers. *121St ASEE Annual Conference & Exposition*, 15–18 June, Indianapolis, IN. doi:10.18260/1-2-23192.

Mercier, E., Tardif, P.A., Moore, L., et al. (2017). Invitations received from potential predatory publishers and fraudulent conferences: A 12-month early-career researcher experience. *Postgraduate Medical Journal* 94(1108): 104–108. doi:10.1136/postgradmedj-2017-135097.

Meyer, C., & Birdsall, N. (2013). *New estimates of india's middle class*. Washington, DC: Center for Global Development.

Moher, D., Shamseer, L., Cobey, K.D., et al., (2017). Stop this waste of people, animals and money. *Nature* 549: 23–25. doi:10.1038/549023a.

Moher, D., & Srivastava, A. (2015). You are invited to submit... *BMC Medicine* 13: 180. doi:10.1186/s12916-015-0423-3.

Nature Editorial. (2018). Journal blacklists: Show your working. *Nature* 562: 308. doi:10.1038/d41586-018-07033-5.

Olijhoek, T., Mitchell, D., & Bjørnshauge, L. (2015). Criteria for open access and publishing. *ScienceOpen Research* 1–8. doi:10.14293/s2199-1006.1.sor-edu.amhuhv.v1.

Perkel, J.M. (2015). Rate that journal. *Nature* 520: 119–120. doi:10.1038/520119a.

Prasad, R. (2017). Cabell's: "Our journal blacklist differs from Jeffrey Beall's". *The Hindu*, 17 June. www.thehindu.com/sci-tech/science/cabells-our-journal-blacklist-differs-from-jeffrey-bealls/article19094374.ece.

Pyne, D. (2017). The rewards of predatory publications at a small business school. *Journal of Scholarly Publishing* 48(3): 137–160. doi:10.3138/jsp.48.3.137.

Shen, C., & Björk, B.C. (2015). "Predatory" open access: A longitudinal study of article volumes and market characteristics. *BMC Medicine* 13: 230. doi:10.1186/s12916-015-0469-2.

Strinzel, M., Severin, A., Milzow, K., et al. (2019). Blacklists and whitelists to tackle predatory publishing: A cross-sectional comparison and thematic analysis. *mBio* 10: e00411–e00419. doi:10.1128/mBio.00411-19.

Sun, L. (2019). Journals removed from DOAJ appearing within SCImago's ranks: A study of excluded journals. *Learned Publishing* 32(3): 207–211. doi:10.1002/leap.1216.

Tao, T. (2020). India's fight against predatory journals: An interview with professor Bhushan Patwardhan. *The Scholarly Kitchen*, 5 February. https://scholarlykitchen.sspnet.org/2020/02/05/indias-fight-against-predatory-journals-an-interview-with-professor-bhushan-patwardhan/.

Teixeira da Silva, J.A. (2013). Predatory publishing: A quantitative assessment, the predatory score. *Asian Australian Journal of Plant Science and Biotechnology* 7: 21–34.

Teixeira da Silva, J.A. (2017). Caution with the continued use of Jeffrey Beall's "predatory" open access publishing lists. *AME Medical Journal* 2(97). doi:10.21037/amj.2017.06.14.

Teixeira da Silva, J.A. (2020). Cabell's International publishing blacklist: An interview with Kathleen Berryman. *Journal of Radical Librarianship* 6: 16–23.

Teixeira da Silva, J.A., & Al-Khatib, A. (2017). The macro and micro scale of open access predation. *Public Research Quarterly* 33: 92–100. doi:10.1007/s12109-016-9495-y.

Teixeira da Silva, J.A., & Tsigaris, P. (2018). What value do journal whitelists and blacklists have in academia? *Journal of Academic Librarianship* 44(6): 781–792. doi:10.1016/j.acalib.2018.09.017.

Thorne, S., Chinn, P.L., Nicoll, L.H., et al. (2014). Predatory publishing. *Journal of Midwifery & Women's Health* 59(6): 569–571. doi:10.1111/jmwh.12273.

Toutloff, L. (2019). Cabells predatory report criteria v 1.1. *The Source*, 20 March. https://blog.cabells.com/2019/03/20/predatoryreport-criteria-v1-1/.

van Gerestein, D. (2015). Quality open access market and other initiatives: A comparative analysis. *LIBER Quarterly* 24(4): 162–173. doi:10.18352/lq.9911.

Walters, W.H. (2016). Information sources and indicators for the assessment of journal reputation and impact. *The Reference Librarian* 57(1): 13–22. doi:10.1080/02763877.2015.1088426.

Xia, J. (2014a). An examination of two Indian megajournals. *Learned Publishing* 27(3): 195–200. doi:10.1087/20130305.

Xia, J. (2014b). Predatory journals and their article processing charges. *Learned Publishing* 28(1): 69–74. doi:10.1087/20150111.

Xu, J., Wang, Z., & Tang, W. (2020). Who published in Chinese predatory journals? A study on the authorship of blacklist journals. *iConference 2020 Proceedings*. http://hdl.handle.net/2142/106529.

4 Publishers

Akça, S., & Akbulut, M. (2018). Predatory journals in Turkey: An investigation through Beall list. *Bilgi Dünyası* 19: 255–274. doi:10.15612/BD.2018.695.

Barrington, D., Shaylor, E., & Sindall, R. (2020). "What the F?": How we failed to publish a journal special issue on failures. *Wash Research*, 15 June. https://wash.leeds.ac.uk/what-the-f-how-we-failed-to-publish-a-journal-special-issue-on-failures/.

Basken, P. (2017). Why Beall's list died – and what it left unresolved about open access. *The Chronicle of Higher Education*, 12 September. www.chronicle.com/article/why-bealls-list-died-and-what-it-left-unresolved-about-open-access/.

Beall, J. (2010). Update: Predatory open-access scholarly publishers. *The Charleston Advisor* 50, July. https://core.ac.uk/download/pdf/11889189.pdf.

Beall, J. (2012). Predatory publishers are corrupting open access. *Nature* 489(7415): 179. doi:10.1038/489179a.

Beall, J. (2013a). Predatory publishing is just one of the consequences of gold open access. *Learned Publishing* 26(2): 79–84. doi:10.1087/20130203.

References

Beall, J. (2013b). Hindawi's profit margin is higher than Elsevier's. *Scholarlyoa. org*, 4 April. http://scholarlyoa.com/2013/04/04/hindawis-profits-are-larger-than-elseviers/.

Beall, J. (2014a). Under pressure, MDPI tries to clean house, retracts paper. *Scholarlyoa.org*, 1 July. https://web.archive.org/web/20140701123905/http://scholarlyoa.com/2014/02/24/under-pressure-mdpi-tries-to-clean-house-retracts-paper/#more-3119.

Beall, J. (2014b). Chinese publisher MDPI added to list of questionable publishers. *Scholarlyoa.org*, 27 February. http://scholarlyoa.com/2014/02/18/chinese-publishner-mdpi-added-to-list-of-questionable-publishers/.

Beall, J. (2016a). Hyderabad, India – city of corruption. *Emerald City Journal*, 22 November. www.emeraldcityjournal.com/2016/11/hyderabad-india-city-of-corruption/.

Beall, J. (2016b). MedCrave update: It's still a dangerous, predatory publisher. *Scholarlyoa.org*, 3 November. https://scholarlyoa.com/2016/11/03/medcrave-update-its-still-a-dangerous-predatory-publisher/.

Beall, J. (2017). What I learned from predatory publishers. *Biochemia Medica* 27(2): 273–278. doi:10.11613/BM.2017.029.

Bohannon, J. (2013). Who's afraid of peer review? *Science* 342(6154): 60–65. doi:10.1126/science.342.6154.60.

Bolshete, P. (2018). Analysis of thirteen predatory publishers: A trap for eager-to-publish researchers. *Current Medical Research and Opinion* 34(1): 157–162. doi: 10.1080/03007995.2017.1358160.

Butler, D. (2013). Investigating journals: The dark side of publishing. *Nature* 495(7442): 433–435. doi:10.1038/495433a.

Cohen, H. (2015). Predatory publishers criticised for "unethical, unprincipled" tactics. *Background Briefing*, 2 August. www.abc.net.au/radionational/programs/backgroundbriefing/predatory-publishers-criticised-unethical-unprincipled-tactics/6656122.

Crawford, W. (2017). Gray OA 2012–2016: Open access journals beyond DOAJ. *Cites & Insights* 17(1): 1–68. http://citesandinsights.info/civ17i1.pdf.

Cyranoski, D. (2018a). China awaits controversial blacklist of "poor quality" journals. *Nature* 562: 471–472. doi:10.1038/d41586-018-07025-5.

Cyranoski, D. (2018b). China introduces "social" publishments for scientific misconduct. *Nature* 564: 312. doi:10.1038/d41586-018-07740-z.

Demir, S.B. (2018). Predatory journals: Who publishes in them and why? *Journal of Informetrics* 12(4): 1296–1311. doi:0.1016/j.joi.2018.10.008.

Deprez, E.E., & Chen, C. (2017). Medical journals have a fake news problem. *Bloomberg Businessweek*, 29 August. www.bloomberg.com/news/features/2017-08-29/medical-journals-have-a-fake-news-problem.

de Vrieze, J. (2018). Open-access journal editors resign after alleged pressure to publish mediocre papers. *Science*, 4 September. doi:10.1126/science.aav3129.

Erfanmanesh, M., & Pourhossein, R. (2017). Publishing in predatory open access journals: A case of Iran. *Publishing Research Quarterly* 33(4): 433–444. doi:10.1007/s12109-017-9547-y.

Hedding, D.W. (2019). Payouts push professors towards predatory journals. *Nature* 565: 267. doi:10.1038/d41586-019-00120-1.

Hegde, A., & Patil, N. (2021). Predatory publishing in India: Has the system failed us? *Acta Neurochirurgica* 163(1): 9–10. doi:0.1007/s00701-020-04644-8.

Hostetler, B. (2020). FTC enforcement: What is equitable relief? *JD Supra*, 5 October. www.jdsupra.com/legalnews/ftc-enforcement-what-is-equitable-relief-70092/.

Jaffé, R. (2020). QUALIS: The journal ranking system undermining the impact of Brazilian science. *Anais da Academia Brasileira de Ciências* 92(3). doi:10.1590/0001-3765202020201116.

Jump, P. (2014). Rejected work gets back in the line-up. *Times Higher Education* 2164. ProQuest document ID: 1552838079.

Kaiser, J. (2013). U.S. government accuses open access publisher of trademark infringement. *Science*, 9 May. www.sciencemag.org/news/2013/05/us-government-accuses-open-access-publisher-trademark-infringement.

Kasprak, A. (2017). *Allegedly legitimate journal publishes "case study" based entirely on a "Seinfeld" episode*. www.snopes.com/news/2017/04/13/science-journal-seinfeld-episode/.

Kaye, D.H. (2017). *The manuscripts of MedCrave*. http://flakyj.blogspot.com/2017/04/the-manuscripts-of-medcrave.html.

Lin, S., & Zhan, L. (2014). Trash journals in China. *Learned Publishing* 27(2): 145–154. doi:10.1087/20140208.

Macháček, V., & Srholec, M. (2021). Predatory publishing in Scopus: Evidence on cross-country differences. *Scientometrics* 126: 1897–1921. doi:10.1007/s11192-020-03852-4.

Manatt, P. (2020). Split ninth circuit upholds $50M FTC victory against online publisher. *JD Supra*, 23 September. www.jdsupra.com/legalnews/split-ninth-circuit-upholds-50m-ftc-39830/.

Manley, S. (2019). Predatory journals on trials: Allegations, responses, and lessons for scholarly publishing from *FTC v. OMICS*. *Journal of Scholarly Publishing* 50(3): 183–200. doi:10.3138/jsp.50.3.02.

Manley, S. (2020). Streaming live – oral arguments in FTC v. OMICS. *The Scholarly Kitchen*, 5 June. https://scholarlykitchen.sspnet.org/2020/06/05/guest-post-streaming-live-oral-arguments-in-ftc-v-omics/.

McCook, A. (2017). Multiple OMICS journals delisted from major index over concerns. *Retraction Watch*, 27 March. https://retractionwatch.com/2017/03/27/multiple-omics-journals-delisted-major-index-concerns.

MDPI. (2014). *Update: Response to Mr. Jeffrey Beall's repeated attacks on MDPI*. www.mdpi.com/about/announcements/534.

Medium.com. (2018). *Aware fake news of medcrave predatory publisher*. https://medium.com/@hector90thorsen/rumours-about-medcrave-predatory-publisher-list-d4c85616b015.

Mouton, J., & Valentine, A. (2017). The extent of South African authored articles in predatory journals. *South African Journal of Science* 113(7–8). doi:10.17159/sajs.2017/20170010.

Naidu, E., & Dell, S. (2019). South Africa: Predatory journals in the firing line. *University World News*, 31 May. www.universityworldnews.com/post.php?story=20190531111556458.

New, J. (2013). Publisher threatens to sue blogger for $1-billion. *The Chronicle of Higher Education*, 15 May. https://www-chronicle-com.proxy.libraries.rutgers.edu/article/publisher-threatens-to-sue-blogger-for-1-billion/.

Patwardhan, B. (2019). Why India is striking back against predatory journals. *Nature* 571: 7. doi:10.1038/d41586-019-02023-7.

Perlin, M.S., Imasato, T., & Borenstein, D. (2018). Is predatory publishing a real threat? Evidence from a large database study. *Scientometrics* 116: 255–273. doi:10.1007/s11192-018-2750-6.

Petrou, C. (2020). MDPI's remarkable growth. *The Scholarly Kitchen*, 10 August. https://scholarlykitchen.sspnet.org/2020/08/10/guest-post-mdpis-remarkable-growth/.

Priyadarshini, S. (2018). India targets universities in predatory-journal crackdown. *Nature* 560: 537–538. doi:10.1038/d41586-018-06048-2.

Reichart, D. (2017). *MedCrave exposed (2017)*. www.danreichart.com/medcrave.

Reynold, W. (Translator). (2020). Indonesia publishes the most open-access journals in the world: What it means for local research. *The Conversation*, 6 October. https://theconversation.com/indonesia-publishes-the-most-open-access-journals-in-the-world-what-it-means-for-local-research-147421.

Sabarini, P. (2021). Indonesia should stop pushing its academics to chase empty indicators. *NIKKEI Asia*, 12 March. https://asia.nikkei.com/Opinion/Indonesia-should-stop-pushing-its-academics-to-chase-empty-indicators.

Schneider, L. (2017). Frontiers: Vanquishers of Beall, publishers of bunk. *Better Science*, 18 September. https://forbetterscience.com/2017/09/18/frontiers-vanquishers-of-beall-publishers-of-bunk/.

Shamseer, L., Moher, D., Maduekwe, O., et al. (2017). Potential predatory and legitimate biomedical journals: Can you tell the difference? A cross-sectional comparison. *BMC Medicine* 15: 28. doi:10.1186/s12916-017-0785-9.

Shen, C., & Björk, B.C. (2015). "Predatory" open access: A longitudinal study of article volumes and market characteristics. *BMC Medicine* 13(1): 230. doi:10.1186/s12916-015-0469-2.

Sriram, J. (2015). SC strikes down "draconian" Section 66A. *The Hindu*, 24 March. www.thehindu.com/news/national/supreme-court-strikes-down-section-66-a-of-the-it-act-finds-it-unconstitutional/article10740659.ece.

Stratford, M. (2012). "Predatory" online journals lure scholars who are eager to publish. *The Chronicle of Higher Education*, 4 March. https://www-chronicle-com.proxy.libraries.rutgers.edu/article/predatory-online-journals-lure-scholars-who-are-eager-to-publish/.

Tao, T. (2020). India's fight against predatory journals: An interview with professor Bhushan Patwardhan. *The Scholarly Kitchen*, 5 February. https://scholarlykitchen.sspnet.org/2020/02/05/indias-fight-against-predatory-journals-an-interview-with-professor-bhushan-patwardhan/.

U.S. District Court. (2019). *Case 2:16-cv-02022-GMN-VCF, Document 121*. www.courthousenews.com/wp-content/uploads/2019/04/Publishing.pdf.

Vervoort, D., Ma, X., & Shrime, M.G. (2020). Money down the drain: Predatory publishing in the COVID-19 era. *Canadian Journal of Public Health* 111: 665–666. doi:10.17269/s41997-020-00411-5.

Wallace, F.H., & Perri, T.J. (2018). Economists behaving badly: Publications in predatory journals. *Scientometrics* 115: 749–766. doi:10.1007/s11192-018-2690-1.

Xia, J., Harmon, J.L., Connolly, K.G., et al. (2015). Who publishes in "predatory" journals? *JASIS&T: Journal of the Association for Information Science and Technology* 66(7): 1406–1417. doi:10.1002/asi.23265.

Yadav, S. (2018). Fake science: Face behind biggest of all – "40 countries, million articles". *The Indian Express*, 22 July. https://indianexpress.com/article/india/face-behind-biggest-of-all-40-countries-million-articles-fake-research-srinubabu-gedela-omics-5266830/.

5 Stakeholders

Al-Khatib, A. (2016). Protecting authors from predatory journals and publishers. *Publishing Research Quarterly* 32: 281–285. doi:10.1007/s12109-016-9474-3.

Anderson, R. (2019). Citation contamination: References to predatory journals in the legitimate scientific literature. *The Scholarly Kitchen*, 28 October. https://scholarlykitchen.sspnet.org/2019/10/28/citation-contamination-references-to-predatory-journals-in-the-legitimate-scientific-literature/.

Bagues, M., Sylos-Labinib, M., & Zinovyeva, N. (2019). A walk on the wild side: "Predatory" journals and information asymmetries in scientific evaluations. *Research Policy* 48: 462–477. doi:10.1016/j.respol.2018.04.013.

Beall, J. (2017). What I learned from predatory publishers. *Biochemia Medica* 27(2): 273–278. doi:10.11613/BM.2017.029.

Björk, B.C., Kanto-Karvonen, S., & Harviainen, J.T. (2020). How frequently are articles in predatory open access journals cited. *Publications* 8(17). doi:10.3390/publications8020017.

Butler, D. (2013). Sham journals scam authors. *Nature* 495: 421–422. doi:10.1038/495421a.

Chambers, A.H. (2019). How I became easy prey to a predatory publisher. *Science*, 9 May. doi:10.1126/science.caredit.aax9725.

Council of Science Editors. (2020). *Editor roles and responsibilities*, updated July. www.councilscienceeditors.org/resource-library/editorial-policies/white-paper-on-publication-ethics/2-1-editor-roles-and-responsibilities/.

Downes, M. (2020). Thousands of Australian academics on the editorial boards of journals run by predatory publishers. *Learned Publishing* 33(3): 287–295. doi:10.1002/leap.1297.

Eaton, S.E. (2018). Who falls prey to predatory publishers? *Learning, Teaching and Leadership*. https://drsaraheaton.wordpress.com.

References

Erfanmanesh, M., & Pourhossein, R. (2017). Publishing in predatory open access journals: A case of Iran. *Publishing Research Quarterly* 33(4): 433–444. doi:10.1007/s12109-017-9547-y.

Fenner, M. (2013). What can article-level metrics do for you? *PLoS Biology* 11(10): e1001687. doi:10.1371/journal.pbio.1001687.

Frandsen, T.F. (2017). Are predatory journals undermining the credibility of science? A bibliometric analysis of citers. *Scientometrics* 113(3): 1513–1528. doi:10.1007/s11192-017-2520-x.

Frandsen, T.F. (2019). Why do researchers decide to publish in questionable journals? A review of the literature. *Learned Publishing* 32(1): 57–62. doi:10.1002/leap.1214.

Kozok, U. (2017). *Predatory publishing: A case story*. https://ipll.manoa.hawaii.edu/internal/documents/predatory-publishers/.

Kozok, U. (2020). *IJARAzerbaijan*. https://ipll.manoa.hawaii.edu/internal/documents/predatory-publishers/ijar-azerbaijan/.

Kurt, S. (2018). Why do authors publish in predatory journals? *Learned Publishing* 31(2): 141–147. doi:10.1002/leap.1150.

Marcus, A., & Oransky, I. (2016). Why fake data when you can fake a scientist? *Nautil* 042. http://nautil.us/issue/42/fakes/why-fake-data-when-you-can-fake-a-scientist.

Moher, D., Shamseer, L., Cobey, K.D., et al. (2017). Stop this waste of people, animals and money. *Nature* 549: 23–25. doi:10.1038/549023a.

NDR. (2018). *More than 5,000 German scientists have published papers in pseudo-scientific journals*. www.ndr.de/der_ndr/presse/More-than-5000-German-scientists-have-published-papers-in-pseudo-scientific-journals,fakescience178.html.

Noga-Styron, K.E., Olivero, J.M., & Britto, S. (2017). Predatory journals in the criminal justices sciences: Getting our cite on the target. *Journal of Criminal Justice Education* 28(2): 174–191. doi:10.1080/10511253.2016.1195421.

Nwagwu, W.E. (2016). Open access in the developing regions: Situating the altercations about predatory publishing. *Canadian Journal of Information and Library Science* 40(1): 58–80.

Omobowale, A.O., Akanle, O., Adeniran, A.I., et al. (2014). Peripheral scholarship and the context of foreign paid publishing in Nigeria. *Current Sociology* 62(5): 666–684. doi:10.1177/0011392113508127.

Perlin, M.S., Imasato, T., & Borenstein, D. (2018). Is predatory publishing a real threat? Evidence from a large database study. *Scientometrics* 116(1): 255–273. doi:10.1007/s11192-018-2750-6.

Pyne, D. (2017). The rewards of predatory publications at a small business school. *Journal of Scholarly Publishing* 48(3): 137–160. doi:10.3138/jsp.48.3.137.

Rawas, H., de Beer, J., Najjar, H.L., et al. (2020). Falling prey to predatory journals: Experiences of nursing faculty. *International Journal of Africa Nursing Sciences* 13. doi:10.1016/j.ijans.2020.100222.

Ray, M. (2016). An expanded approach to evaluating open access journals. *Journal of Scholarly Publishing* 47(4): 307–326. doi:10.3138/jsp.47.4.307.

Ruiter-Lopez, L., Lopez-Leonb, S., & Forero, D.A. (2019). Predatory journals: Do not judge journals by their editorial board members. *Medical Teacher* 41(6): 691–696. doi:10.1080/0142159X.2018.1556390.

Seethapathy, G.S., Santhosh Kumar, J.U., & Hereesha, A.S. (2016). India's scientific publication in predatory journals: Need for regulating quality of Indian science and education. *Current Science* 111(11): 1759–1764. doi:10.18520/cs/v111/i11/1759-1764.

Severin, A., Strinzel, M., Egger, M., et al. (2020). Who reviews for predatory journals? A study on reviewer characteristics. *BioRxiv*, 11 March. doi:10.1101/2020.03.09.983155.

Shaw, C. (2013). Hundreds of open access journals accept fake science paper. *The Guardian*, 4 October. www.theguardian.com/higher-education-network/2013/oct/04/open-access-journals-fake-paper.

Shen, C., & Björk, B.C. (2015). "Predatory" open access: A longitudinal study of article volumes and market characteristics. *BMC Medicine* 13(1): 230. doi:10.1186/s12916-015-0469-2.

Shuva, N.Z., & Taisir, R. (2016). Faculty members' perceptions and use of open access journals: Bangladesh perspective. *International Federation of Library Associations and Institutions* 42(1): 36–48. doi:10.1177/0340035216628879.

Sorokowski, P., Kulczycki, M., Sorokowska, A., et al. (2017). Predatory journals recruit fake editor. *Nature* 543(7646): 481–483. doi:10.1038/543481a.

Stratford, M. (2012). "Predatory" online journals lure scholars who are eager to publish. *The Chronicle of Higher Education*, 4 March. https://www-chronicle-com.proxy.libraries.rutgers.edu/article/Predatory-Online-Journals/131047.

Truth, F. (2012). Pay big to publish fast: Academic journal rackets. *Journal for Critical Education Policy Studies* 10(2): 54–105.

Van Noorden, R. (2020). Hundreds of scientists have peer-reviewed for predatory journals. *Nature*, 11 March. doi:10.1038/d41586-020-00709-x.

Wallace, F.H., & Perri, T.J. (2018). Economists behaving badly: Publications in predatory journals. *Scientometrics* 115: 749–766. doi:10.1007/s11192-018-2690-1.

Xia, J. (2019). Economic modelling of predatory journal publishing. *Publishing Research Quarterly* 35(3): 377–390. doi:10.1007/s12109-019-09661-9.

Xia, J., Harmon, J.L., Connolly, K.G., et al. (2015). Who publishes in "predatory" journals? *JASIS&T: Journal of the Association for Information Science and Technology* 66(7): 1406–1417. doi:10.1002/asi.23265.

Xu, J., Wang, Z., & Tang, W. (2020). Who published in Chinese predatory journals? A study on the authorship of blacklist journals. *iConference 2020 Proceedings*. http://hdl.handle.net/2142/106529.

6 Hijacked publishing

Abalkina, A. (2020a). Detecting a network of hijacked journals by its archive. *arXiv*. https://arxiv.org/ftp/arxiv/papers/2101/2101.01224.pdf.

References

Abalkina, A. (2020b). The case of the stolen journal. *Retraction Watch*, 7 July. https://retractionwatch.com/2020/07/07/the-case-of-the-stolen-journal/.

Al-Amr, M. (2020). How did content from a hijacked journal end up in one of the world's most-used databases? *Retraction Watch*, 1 September. https://retractionwatch.com/2020/09/01/how-did-content-from-a-hijacked-journal-end-up-in-one-of-the-worlds-most-used-databases.

Bohannon, J. (2015). Feature: How to hijack a journal. *Science*, 19 November. doi:10.1126/science.aad7463.

Bravo-Vinaja, A. (2017). Hijacked journals in agricultural sciences and related areas. *Revista Fitotecnia Mexicana* 40(3): 241–248.

Butler, D. (2013). Sham journals scam authors. *Nature* 495(7442): 421–422. doi:10.1038/495421a.

Dadkhah, M., & Borchardt, G. (2016). Hijacked journals: An emerging challenge for scholarly publishing. *Aesthetic Surgery Journal* 36(6): 739–741. doi:10.1093/asj/sjw026.

Dadkhah, M., Maliszewski, T., & Teixeira da Silva, J.A. (2016a). Hijacked journals, hijacked web-sites, journal phishing, misleading metrics, and predatory publishing: Actual and potential threats to academic integrity and publishing ethics. *Forensic Science, Medicine, and Pathology* 12: 353–362. doi:10.1007/s12024-016-9785-x.

Dadkhah, M., Maliszewski, T., & Lyashenko, V. (2016b). An approach for preventing the indexing of hijacked journal articles in scientific databases. *Behaviour & Information Technology* 35(4): 298–303. doi:10.1080/0144929X.2015.1128975.

Dadkhah, M., Seno, S.A.H., & Borchardt, G. (2017a). Current and potential cyber attacks on medical journals: Guidelines for improving security. *European Journal of Internal Medicine* 38: 25–29. doi:10.1016/j.ejim.2016.11.014.

Dadkhah, M., Lagzian, M., & Borchardt, G. (2017b). Questionable papers in citation databases as an issue for literature review. *Journal of Cell Communication and Signaling* 11: 181–185. doi:10.1007/s12079-016-0370-6.

Dadkhah, M., Sutikno, T., Jazi, M.D., et al. (2015). An introduction to journal phishings and their detection approach. *Telkomnika* 13: 373–380.

Jalalian, M. (2014). Journal hijackers target science and open access. *Research Information*, 11 August. www.researchinformation.info/analysis-opinion/journal-hijackers-target-science-and-open-access.

Jalalian, M., & Dadkhah, M. (2015). The full story of 90 hijacked journals from August 2011 to June 2015. *Geographica Pannonica* 19(2): 73–87. doi:10.18421/GP19.02-06.

Jalalian, M., & Mahboobi, H. (2014). Hijacked journals and predatory publishers: Is there a need to rethink how to assess the quality of academic research? *Walailak Journal of Science and Technology* 11(5): 389–394. doi:10.14456/wjst.2014.16.

Lukić, T., Blešić, I., Basarin, B., et al. (2014). Predatory and fake scientific journals/publishers – a global outbreak with rising trend: A review. *Geographica Pannonica* 18(3): 69–81.

Memon, A.R. (2019). Hijacked journals: A challenge unaddressed to the developing world. *Journal of the Pakistan Medical Association* 69(10): 1413–1415.

Pollock, D. (2020). News & views: Open access market sizing update 2020. *Delta Think*, 19 October. https://deltathink.com/news-views-open-access-market-sizing-update-2020/.

Shahri, M.A., Jazi, M.D., Borchardt, G., et al. (2018). Detecting hijacked journals by using classification algorithms. *Science and Engineering Ethics* 24: 655–668. doi:10.1007/s11948-017-9914-2.

7 Conferences

Asadi, A., Rahbar, N., Asadi, M., et al. (2017). Online-based approaches to identify real journals and publishers from hijacked ones. *Science and Engineering Ethics* 23(1): 305–308. doi:10.1007/s11948-017-9906-2.

Bartneck, C. (2016). iOS just got a paper on nuclear physics accepted at a scientific conference. *Personal Blog*, 20 October. www.bartneck.de/2016/10/20/ios-just-got-a-paper-on-nuclear-physics-accepted-at-a-scientific-conference/.

Brooks, M. (2009). Red-flag conferences. *The Chronicle of Higher Education*, 26 March. www.chronicle.com/article/red-flag-conferences/.

Cobey, K.D., de Costa e Silva, M., Mazzarello, S., et al. (2017). Is this conference for real? Navigating presumed predatory conference invitations. *Journal of Oncology Practice* 13(7): 410–414. doi:10.1200/JOP.2017.021469.

Cohen, J. (2013). Meetings that flatter, but may not deliver. *Science* 342(6154): 76–77. doi:10.1126/science.342.6154.76.

Chapman, S. (2016). Philip Morris speaks at and promotes an obscure conference on lung disease. *The Conversation*, 18 July. https://theconversation.com/philip-morris-speaks-at-and-promotes-an-obscure-conference-on-lung-disease-62497.

Cress, P.E. (2017). Are predatory conferences the dark side of the open access movement? *Aesthetic Surgery Journal* 37(6): 734–738. doi:10.1093/asj/sjw247.

Deprez, E.E., & Chen, C. (2017). Medical journals have a fake news problem. *Bloomberg Businessweek*, 29 August. www.bloomberg.com/news/features/2017-08-29/medical-journals-have-a-fake-news-problem.

Eckert, S., Krause, T., & Sumner, C. (2018). Inside the fake science factory. *The Def Con*, 11 August. Las Vegas. https://media.defcon.org/DEF%20CON%2026/DEF%20CON%2026%20presentations/DEFCON-26-Eckert-Sumner-Krause-Inside-the-Fake-Science-Factory-Updated.pdf.

Fedele, R. (2019). Nurse academics warned to look out for conference scams. *Australian Nursing & Midwifery Journal*, 13 March. https://anmj.org.au/nurse-academics-warned-to-look-out-for-conference-scams/.

Federal Trade Commission. (2019). *OMICS Group Inc*. Last Updated: 15 October 2019. www.ftc.gov/enforcement/cases-proceedings/152-3113/federal-trade-commission-v-omics-group-inc.

References

Foxx, A.J., Barak, R.S., Lichtenberger, T.M., et al. (2019). Evaluating the prevalence and quality of conference codes of conduct. *PNAS* 116(30): 14931–14936. doi:10.1073/pnas.1819409116.

Gillis, A. (2018). Poor-quality, predatory conferences prey on academics. *University Affairs*, 5 March. www.universityaffairs.ca/news/news-article/poor-quality-predatory-conferences-prey-academics/.

Grove, J. (2017). Predatory conferences now outnumber official scholarly events. *Times Higher Education*, 26 October. www.timeshighereducation.com/news/predatory-conferences-now-outnumber-official-scholarly-events.

Heasman, P.A. (2019). Unravelling the mysteries of predatory conferences. *British Dental Journal* 226: 228–230. doi:10.1038/sj.bdj.2019.101.

Ika, S. (2015). Flaky academic conferences. *Forensic Online Course*, 24 December. http://forensiconlinecourseinfo.blogspot.com/2015/12/flaky-academic-conferences.html.

Kolata, G. (2013). Scientific articles accepted (personal checks, too). *The New York Times*, 7 April. www.nytimes.com/2013/04/08/health/for-scientists-an-exploding-world-of-pseudo-academia.html?pagewanted=all&_r=0.

Kscien Organization. (2021). *Predatory conferences*. http://kscien.org/predatory.php?id=7.

Kulamer, B., Meester, W., Salk, J., et al. (2017). Recommended practices to ensure technical conference content quality. *Science Editor and Publisher* 2(1): 47–51. doi:10.24069/2542-0267-2017-1-1-12.

Lang, R., Mintz, M., Krentz, H.B., et al. (2019). An approach to conference selection and evaluation: Advice to avoid "predatory" conferences. *Scientometrics* 118: 687–698. doi:10.1007/s11192-018-2981-6.

Mackenzie, R.J. (2019). Inside a "fake" conference: A journey into predatory science. *Technology Networks*, 11 July. www.technologynetworks.com/tn/articles/inside-a-fake-conference-a-journey-into-predatory-science-321619.

McCrostie, J. (2016). Taiwan's great academic rip-off. *Taipei Times*, 3 August. www.taipeitimes.com/News/feat/archives/2016/08/03/2003652340.

McCrostie, J. (2017). Developing criteria for identifying predatory conferences. *Bulletin of Daito Bunka University* LV: 179–188.

McCrostie, J. (2020). Our predatory conference problem. In *Corruption in higher education: Global challenges and responses*, edited by E. Denisova-Schmidt. Leiden: Brill Publishers, pp. 43–48.

McMillin, D. (2019). What to do about fake and predatory conferences. *PCMA*, 1 October. www.pcma.org/fake-predatory-conferences/.

Memon, A.R., & Azim, M.E. (2018). Predatory conferences: Addressing researchers from developing countries. *Journal of the Pakistan Medical Association* 68(11): 1691–1695.

Mercier, E., Tardif, P.A., Moore, L., et al. (2018). Invitations received from potential publishers and fraudulent conferences: A 12-month early-career researcher experience. *Postgraduate Medical Journal* 94(1): 104–108. doi:10.1136/postgradmedj-2017-135097.

Mertkan, S., Aliusta, G.O., & Suphi, N. (2021). Knowledge production on predatory publishing: A systematic review. *Learned Publishing*, Early view. doi:10.1002/leap.1380.

Nisha, F., Das, A.K., & Tripathi, M. (2020). Stemming the rising tide of predatory journals and conferences: A selective review of literature. *Annals of Library and Information Studies* 67(3): 173–182.

Oberhaus, D. (2018). Hundreds of researchers from Harvard, Yale and Stanford were published in fake academic journals. *VICE*, 14 August. www.vice.com/en/article/3ky45y/hundreds-of-researchers-from-harvard-yale-and-stanford-were-published-in-fake-academic-journals.

Pai, M., & Franco, E. (2016). Predatory conferences undermine science and scam academics. *Huffington Post*, 13 October. www.huffingtonpost.ca/dr-madhukar-pai/predatory-conferences-academia_b_12467834.html.

Ruben, A. (2016). Dubious conferences put the "pose" in "symposium". *Science*, 23 November. doi:10.1126/science.caredit.a1600157.

8 Metrics and indexes

Archambault, É., & Larivière, V. (2009). History of the journal impact factor: Contingencies and consequences. *Scientometrics* 79(3): 639–653. doi:10.1007/s11192-007-2036-x.

Casadevall, A., & Fang, F.C. (2014). Causes for the persistence of impact factor mania. *mBio* 5(2): e00064-14. doi:10.1128/mBio.00064-14.

Dadkhah, M., Maliszewski, T., & Jazi, M.D. (2016). Characteristics of hijacked journals and predatory publishers: Our observations in the academic world. *Trends in Pharmacological Sciences* 37(6): 415–418. doi:10.1016/j.tips.2016.04.002.

Erfanmanesh, M. (2017). Status and quality of open access journals in Scopus. *Collection Building* 36(4): 155–162. doi:10.1108/CB-02-2017-0007.

Gutierrez, F.R.S., Beall, J., & Forero, D.A. (2015). Spurious alternative impact factors: The scale of the problem from an academic perspective. *BioEssays* 37(5): 474–476. doi:10.1002/bies.201500011.

Jalalian, M. (2015). The story of fake impact factor companies and how we detected them. *Electron Physician* 7(2): 1069–1072. doi:10.14661/2015.1069-1072.

Jalalian, M., & Mahboobi, H. (2013). New corruption detected: Bogus impact factors compiled by fake organizations. *Electronic Physician* 5(3): 685–686. doi:10.14661/2013.685-686.

Lukić, T., Blešić, I., Basarin, B., et al. (2014). Predatory and fake scientific journals/publishers – a global outbreak with rising trend: A review. *Geographica Pannonica* 69(3): 70–96. doi:10.5937/GeoPan1403069L.

McVeigh, M.E. (2004). *Open access journals in the ISI citation databases: Analysis of impact factors and citation patterns – a citation study from Thomson scientific*. http://ip-science.thomsonreuters.com/m/pdfs/openaccesscitations2.pdf.

Seglen, P.O. (1997). Citations and journal impact factors: Questionable indicators of research quality. *Allergy* 52: 1050–1056. doi:10.1111/j.1398-9995.1997.tb00175.x.

Shamseer, L., Moher, D., Maduekwe, O., *et al.* (2017). Potential predatory and legitimate biomedical journals: can you tell the difference? A cross-sectional comparison. *BMC Medicine* 15: 28. doi:10.1186/s12916-017-0785-9.

Shen, C., & Björk, B.C. (2015). "Predatory" open access: A longitudinal study of article volumes and market characteristics. *BMC Medicine* 13(1): 230. doi:10.1186/s12916-015-0469-2.

van Leeuwen, T. (2012). Discussing some basic critique on journal impact factors: Revision of earlier comments. *Scientometrics* 92(2): 443–455. doi:10.1007/s11192-012-0677-x.

Van Noorden, R. (2016). Controversial impact factor gets a heavyweight rival. *Nature* 540: 325–326. doi:10.1038/nature.2016.21131.

van Wesel, M. (2016). Evaluation by citation: Trends in publication behavior, evaluation criteria, and the strive for high impact publications. *Science and Engineering Ethics* 22(1): 199–225. doi:10.1007/s11948-015-9638-0.

Xia, J. (2019). A preliminary study of alternative open access journal indexes. *Publishing Research Quarterly* 35: 274–284. doi:10.1007/s12109-019-09642-y

Xia, J., & Smith, M.P. (2018). Alternative journal impact factors in open access publishing. *Learned Publishing* 31: 403–411. doi:10.1002/leap.1200.

Index

Note: Page numbers in *italics* indicate a figure and page numbers in **bold** indicate a table on the corresponding page.

Abalkina, A. 76, 89
Academia.edu 69
academic community 8, 18, 19, 23, 26, 32, 37, 43, 52, 68, 89, 102
academic conferences 91–92
academic credentials 71, 75
academic credit 72
academic disciplines 23–24, 30, 106
Academic Journal Guide 25
academic misconduct 2, 113, 115
academic rankings 3, 60
academic witch-hunts 4
Academie Royal des Sciences d Outre-Mer Bulletin des Seances 88
Academy of Science of South Africa 56
Afinidad 78, **79**, 86, *86*, 107
African Journal of Pharmacy and Pharmacology 72–73
Alexa database 87
alternative indexes 2, **110**, 111–112
Anderson, R. 73
anti-predatory publishing 54
Archives des Sciences 77, 80, 83–84
article-level metrics 23, 72, 109
article processing charges 14, 30–32
article processing fees (APCs) 1, 6–8, 10–15, 30–31, 33, 44, 48–49, 51–52, 60–61, 70, 75, 78, 80, 83–84, 89, 114
artificial metrics 4, 106–111, **108–109**
Australian academic community 68
Australian Business Deans Council (ABDC) 25, 36

authors: predatory authors 59–63; predatory journals 63–66; sampled authors publishing 45; stakeholders 59–66
authorship: heterogeneous 74; predatory authors 63
automated language analysis technique 33
awareness 3, 24, 37, 55, 101–102, 114–115
Azerbaijan-based business 61
Azim, M.E. 93

Beall, J. 1–2, 11, 27, 39, 41–43, 45, 47–50, 53–54, 76–78, 92, 95; blacklist of standalone predatory journals 13–16; predatory behaviors, criteria for 116–117
beallslist.net 16
behaviors/behavioral: aggressive and unethical 101; indicators 17
Biochemia Medica 89
biomedical publisher 83
Björk, B.C. 2, 29, 32, 45, 59, 73
blacklists: Cabells's blacklist of predatory journals 16–18; cloned 16; in-house 19; journal 2–3; predatory journals 13–19; of publishers, development 39–41, *40–41*; of standalone predatory journals 13–16; and whitelists, comparison 26–29, *27*
Bloomberg Businessweek 51
Bohannon, J. 60, 82–84, 86–87

Index 143

Bolshete, P. 46
Borchardt, G. 89
Brazil 56–57, 94
business: management 1, 14, 25, 36,, 94; operations 15, 28, 43, 109
Butler, D. 83

Cabells Classification Index (CCI) 23
Cabells's blacklist of predatory journals 16–18
Cabells's criteria for predatory practices 118–122
Cabells's whitelist 22–23, 27–28
Canadian business school 63, 65
Chambers, A.H. 64
cheating behaviors 15, 33–34, 112, 114
Chen, C. 17
China 9, 19, 46, 56, 62–63, 72
Chronicle 54
citations 32, 48–50, 55, 60, 72, 88, 109–110
CiteScore 106
Clarivate Analytics 106
cloned blacklists 16
Cobey, K.D. 1, 14, 26, 28–29
co-editor 61, 68
co-existence 42
commercial publishers 7, 42–43
Committee on Publication Ethics (COPE) 36–37
community-curated online index 20
conferences: keynotes, planning committee members and attendees 96–98; medical, predatory 99–100; names 92; online delivery of 104; organizers 95–97; predatory 92–95, 99–103; publications 98–99; -related events 94–95; stakeholders 95–99; themes 98
controversial publishers 39
COPE *see* Committee on Publication Ethics (COPE)
Council on Higher Education 56
Crawford, W. 28–31, 33–35, 43
credit card swiping online 80
crime 4, 75–76, 84, 90
criminal activities, scholarly publishing 115
criminal justice science 64

criminals 75, 77, 115; *see also* cybercriminals
Croatian Society of Medical Biochemistry and Laboratory Medicine 89
crowd-sourced services 26, **26**
Cukier, S. 1
cyber-attacks on journals 80
Cybercrime Coordination Unit Switzerland and Austrian police 84
cybercriminals 79–81, 88, 90
cyber-spoofing 75

Dadkhah, M. 76, 78–79, 81, 85, 87–89
dead journals 35, **35**
Department of Higher Education and Training (DHET) 55
Difficulty of Acceptance metrics 23
Dionne, R. 50
Directory of Open Access Journals (DOAJ) 7, 11, 20–24, 27–28, 36, 45, 49, 60, 69–70, 111–112, 114
disciplinary whitelists 24–26
discipline-specific studies 2
discount rates 31
DOAJ *see* Directory of Open Access Journals
DOAJ, community-curated online index 20
DOAJ Seal 21–22
dominant academic language 59–60
Dony, C. 17
Downes, M. 68

East China University of Political Science and Law (ECUPSL) 19
Eckert, S. 95, 99–100
e-currency transfers 80
editorial boards 2, 12, 15, 41, 48, 53, 59, 68–70, 95, 102
editors: and editorial board members 66–70; publishing services 42; and staff 1
editorship 3, 12, 42, 68, 74
Electronic Physician journal 76
Elsevier 51, 106
email invitations 36, 75, 97
English-language journals 60, 75, 79
Entomological Society of America 92
Entomology-2013 92

144 Index

Eriksson, S. 1, 14–15
Eureka Science 97
Euromed Communications 83
exploitative behaviors 8, 46

fake to lax peer review 15
fake web addresses/websites 77–80, 82, 84, 88
false discoveries 74
false negatives and positives, predatory journals 27
formal publications 12
Frandsen, T.F. 74
Frontiers Media 54
FTC v. OMICS case 52
fundamental conflict 42

Global Impact Factor 34
gold OA 6–7, 28, 75
gold OA journals 6, 28
Google 87; Google+ 69; Google Maps 43–44; Google Scholar 73
go-to tools 2, 43
government actions against predatory publishing 54–57
grab-and-run approach 89
grammar 60
grammatical errors 12, 32, 36, 101
Graphis Scripta 83
gray OA 28, 29
gray OA journal concept 28
Gray OA Universe 28

harassments and legal threats 15–16
Heasman, P.A. 101
Helgesson, G. 1, 14–15
Higher Education Forum 96
high pressure 65
hijacked journal list 76, 79, **79**, 88
Hijacked Journals 2, 76–82, 86–89
hijacked publishing: anonymous professor 81–82; articles 88–89; Boranbaev, Ruslan 80–81; cases 76–80; detecting hijacking 86–88; existing domains, snatching 83; expired domains replacement 82; hijacked journals, identification features **87**; journal list **79**; key hijackers 80–82; print journals advantage 83–84; Robinson, James 81;
tactics 82–86; tricking users with similar domains 84–86
home-grown watchlists and safelists 114
humanities journals 30

imitating legitimate events 91
India 8–11, 24, 31, 45, 47, 49–51, 54–55, 60–61, 63, 72, 95, 98, 109
Indian Express 50
Indian mega-journals 31
Indonesia 45, 56–57, 61
in-house blacklists 19
in-house whitelists 24–26
innocent victims 35–37, 63, 74
Innova Ciencia 80, 82
Institute for Scientific Information (ISI) 106
instruction-oriented institutions/ universities 61, 62
integrity 1, 17, 23–24, 36, 55–56, 102
International Academy of Nursing Editors 26
International Bibliography of the Social Sciences 55
International Business Academics Consortium 96
International Conference of Entomology 92
International Conference on Atomic and Nuclear Physics 100
International Congress and Convention Association (ICCA) 95
International Journal of Clinical Rheumatology 51
International Journal of Game Theory 80
Internet Archive (archive.org) 16
Internet Corporation for Assigned Names and Numbers 86

Jalalian, M. 76, 78–79, 81–82, 84, 89, 107
JIF score 86, 105–106, 111
journal: article processing charges 30–32; blacklists and whitelists, comparison 26–29; card 23; cheating behaviors 33–34; hijacking 88; -level metrics 106; longevity 34–35; open access journals, whitelists

Index 145

19–26; predatory 13–19; predatory publications, volume 29–30, **30**; prefixes **34**; publishing 59; scholarly quality 32–33; spam emails 12–13
Journal Blacklist 2–3, 12–14, 16, 18–19, 28, 42–43, 56, 112
journal impact factor 34, 105, 107
journal impact factor (JIF) scores 34
Journal of Biomedical Sciences 51
Journal of Clinical & Experimental Pharmacology 51
Journal of Contemporary Art 82–83
Journal of Medicinal Plants Research 72–73
Journal of Plant Biotechnology 83
Journal of Preventive Medicine by OMICS 51
Journal of Proteomics & Bioinformatics 50
Journal of the American Medical Association 80
Journal Quality List (JQL) 25, 36; journal ranks in **25**; purpose 25
Journalytics 22–23

Knowledge E 102
Kozok, U. 61, 68
Kscien Organization 95
Kurt, S. 37, 66

Lang, R. 102
legal challenges, publishers 39, 52–54
legitimacy 2, 89, 102, 107, 114
literature 2, 41–42, 54, 59, 63–64, 76, 79, 92, 98, 115
local academic culture 37
longevity 34–35
Ludus Vitalis 83
Lukić, T. 76

Macháček, V. 45
Mahboobi, H. 84, 107
Manley, S. 53
Markowitz, D. 33
McCrostie, J. 92–93, 96, 98, 100
MedCrave 47
mega-journals 29, 31, 111
mega-publishing 67
Memon, A.R. 93

metrics and indexes: alternative indexes 2, **110**, 111–112; artificial metrics 106–111; background 105–106; Journal impact factor (JIF) 34, 105–106
misidentifications 41
misleading metrics 107
Multidisciplinary Digital Publishing Institute (MDPI) 41–42, 47–49, **49**
Murad, F. 97

National Institute of Nursing Research 50
National Institutes of Health (NIH) 33, 50
National Research Foundation 56
networking events 91
New, J. 53
Nigeria: predatory journals based in 71; publishers 72; scholars 65
NIH-funded scientists 50
non-academic editors 67
non-English-speaking countries 84
non-predatory journals 20, 42, 65, 111
non-predatory OA journals 30, 60
non-predatory OA publishers 45
non-publishing businesses 83
Nordic Lichen Society 83
Norwegian Register for Scientific Journals 55
Nurse Author & Editor journal 26
Nwagwu, W.E. 61

OA commercial publisher 41
OA publishers 6, 43, 48–49
OMICS 47, 50–53, 92, 94–101
OMICS International 47, 49–52
OMICS Online Publishing 50
Omobowale, A.O. 64
online or social media discussions 72
open access journals, whitelists: Cabells's whitelist 22–23; crowd-sourced services 26; directory 20–22; in-house whitelists 24–26
open access (OA) movement 3
open-access publishing 45
Open Access Scholarly Publishers' Association (OASPA) 37
Open Journal Systems 46, 78

Index

parasitic conference giants 94
Perlin, M.S. 57
Perri, T.J. 62–63
personal reputation 37, 64
pharmaceutical science 94, 99–100
phishing 88
plagiarism 32, 51
Polish Forestry Society 84
Polish scholars 69
predators 91, 104–106, 114
predatory authors 9, 56, 59–64, **61**, 66; authorship 62–66; in economics **62**
predatory behaviors 17, 42, 64, 104, 113–115
predatory conferences 96; characteristics 92; conference industry, actions by 101–102; list of indicators **93–94**; scale of 94–95; sting operations 100–101
predatory criteria revisited 42–43
predatory editorship 68, 74
predatory journals 42, 64–65; article processing charges 30–32; authors 63–66; blacklists 13–19; characteristics 29–35; cheating behaviors 33–34; editors 45; innocent victims 35–37; longevity 34–35; predatory publications, volume 29–30, **30**; in Qualis 57; scholarly quality 32–33; tips on avoiding 35–37; willing participants 37
predatory medical conferences 99–100
predatory meetings 92
predatory organizers 91, 96, 104
predatory outlets, publishing 3
predatory practices to scholarship 3
predatory publications 3, 6, 10–12, 18–19, 29–30, **30**, 32, 44–45, **44**, 56–57, 62, 65, 72–74, 99, 112
predatory publishers 1–4, 6, 13, 39, *40*, 42, 43–46, 56–57, 61, 66–67, 69, 72, 74–75, 89, 95, 114; IP contact locations 45; practices by 43–52; publishers 52–54
predatory publishing 16, 113–115; definition 1–2; provenance 5–8; quality gatekeeping 10–11
Preventive Medicine 51
profitable publisher 46
pseudoscience articles 47–48, 74

pseudo-scientific journals 63
publishers: blacklist, development of 39–41, *40–41*; Brazil 56–57; business operations, location 43–46; China 56; government actions against predatory publishing 54–57; India 54–55; Indonesia 56–57; legal challenges 52–54; Multidisciplinary Digital Publishing Institute (MDPI) 47–49; OMICS International 49–52; predatory criteria revisited 42–43; predatory publishers 43–54; selected publishers, anatomy 47–52; South Africa 55–56; warehouse publishing 46–47
publishing crime 4
"Publish or Perish" application 88
publish-or-perish 8–9, 60, 113–114
Publons 70–72
PubMed Central 19, 50

Qualis 57

readers 72–74
recognition mechanism 101–102
representative publishers 39
research proficiency 37, 65–66
reviewers 70–72, 74
Robinson, J. 77–78, 81
Royal Society of Chemistry (RSC) events 97

sampled authors publishing 45
scholarly journals 2, 6, 33, 54, 91, 114
Scholarly Open Access 13
scholarly publishing, pressure on 8–10
scholarly quality 28, 32–33, 46–47
SciELO SA 55–56
Science and Nature 77, 82
ScienceDirect database 73
Science Magazine 64, 84
Science Publishing Group 68
Science Series Data Report 77, 82
scientific credibility 64
Scopus 9, 50, 55–56, 73, 75, 86, 88–89, 106, 111
search engine optimization (SEO) techniques 85
Seethapathy, G.S. 61
self-identified publishers 45

Index 147

self-plagiarized paper 50
self-proclaimed international
  conferences 97
self-promotion 71
self-publishing 5
Shamseer, L. 45
Shen, C. 29, 45, 59
single-journal publishers 13, 39, 45, 67
social credit system 56
social identity threat 65–66
social science journals 19, 30
Spain-based journal 78
spam: emails 12–13; invitations 13
Srholec, M. 45
stakeholders: authors 59–66;
  conferences 95–99; editors and
  editorial board members 66–70;
  readers 72–74; reviewers 70–72
standalone journals 13, **14**, 31, 39, 51, 67
Strinzel, M. 26–27
Suber, P. 49
subscription-based access to open
  access 113
suspicious conferences 92
Sustainability 49
Switzerland-based OA publisher 54
Sylwan 84–85, *85*
Szust, A.O. 69–70

Talent Development and Excellence
  88–89
technical conferences 92–93
template journals 46
Texas Journal of Science 82
Think.Check.Attend 102, *103*
Think.Check.Submit 36, 102
third-party websites 35
transparency 2, 16, 57
Twitter 69
Tyagi, P. 51

UGC-CARE 24
UGC-CARE Reference List of Quality
  Journals 55

UlrichWeb 85
Umjetnosti, Z. 82
unawareness 33, 65
unethical practices 29, 37, 42,
  63, 98
Universal Impact Factor 34, 107
University Grants Commission (UGC)
  24, 55, 61
University of Colorado 13
University of Costa Rica 83
University of Liverpool journals 83
unprofessional and unethical
  conduct 75
unwanted emails 13
US Federal Trade Commission (FTC)
  52–53, 95–96

vanity publishing 5–6
Van Noorden, R. 71

Wallace, F.H. 62–63
WASET *see* World Academy
  of Science, Engineering and
  Technology (WASET)
Web of Science (WoS) 9, 19, 25,
  33–36, 47–49, 55–56, 69, 72–73,
  75, 77, 82–84, 86–88, 105–107,
  109, 111–112
web service SCImago Journal &
  Country Rank 86
web-spoofing techniques 77
WEKA 87
WHOIS 86–87, 96
willing participants, predatory journals
  3, 37
wire transfers 80
World Academy of Science,
  Engineering and Technology
  (WASET) 95–96, 98–100
World Bank 63
WoS-indexed journals 35
Wulfenia 77–78, 83–84, 107

Xia, J. 31, 45, 107, 110–112

For Product Safety Concerns and Information please contact our EU representative GPSR@taylorandfrancis.com
Taylor & Francis Verlag GmbH, Kaufingerstraße 24, 80331 München, Germany

www.ingramcontent.com/pod-product-compliance
Lightning Source LLC
Chambersburg PA
CBHW051749230426
43670CB00012B/2215